Using the Case Method to Support Intercultural Learning in Higher Education: Findings from an Indo-German Project

ABOUT THE AUTHORS

Prof. Dr. Matthias Pilz is full professor of Economics and Business Education at the University of Cologne.

Prof. Pilz studied Business Education at the University of Goettingen from 1990 tod 1995 and Economics at the University of Edinburgh/Scotland in 1992-93. From 1996 to 1998, he was research assistant at the Chair of Economic Education at the TU Dresden and received his Doctor's degree/Ph.D. at the University of Konstanz in 1999. After finishing his initial teacher training in 2002, he started his teaching career at the Wirtschaftsschule (Business College) Herrenhausen in Hannover and was simultaneously advisor for EU education projects at the district government of Hannover. In the years 2002 to 2004 he worked as research associate for the Institute of Business Education and Educational Management at The University of St. Gallen/Switzerland before becoming a full professor for general economic studies in pre vocational education at the Freiburg University of Education. Since 2009, he is a full professor at the University of Cologne and Director of the G.R.E.A.T. (German Research Center for Comparative Vocational Education and Training) and since 2010 the CMIS-UC (Center for Modern Indian Studies at the University of Cologne).

His research interests are international comparative research in vocational education and training, research in transition from the education to the employment system as well as research into teaching and learning.

Dipl.-Kffr. Sarah Pierenkemper is research assistant at the Department of Business and Economics Education as well as at the German Research Centre of Comparative Education and Vocational Training at the University of Cologne. Since 2012, she is the executive director of the Center for Modern Indian Studies at the University of Cologne.

Sarah Pierenkemper studied business administration and business education at the University of Cologne, Germany and Teesside University, UK.

In the years 2011 and 2012, Sarah Pierenkemper has been to India by a German Academic Exchange Service (DAAD) research grant to study the Indian vocational education and training system.

Her research interests are in comparative vocational education and training with a special focus on the Indian VET-system.

Dipl.-Hdl. David B. Meinhard is research assistant at the Center for Higher Education Quality (cheQ) at the Faculty of Management, Economics and Social Sciences at the University of Cologne.

He studied business education at the University of Cologne from 2005 to 2010 and at the Universidad de Salamanca, Spain, in 2008-2009 as he participated in an interdisciplinary exchange programme.

After finishing the diploma study programme in 2010 he started working at cheQ in the field of Academic Staff Development. Since then, David was also engaged in the activities of the Center for Modern Indian Studies at the University of Cologne and went to India by a German Academic Exchange Service (DAAD) research grant to study good practices of Academic Staff Development at Indian Universities.

His main research interests are Strategies and Methods of Teaching and Learning in the Business and Management Sciences.

Using the Case Method to Support Intercultural Learning in Higher Education: Findings from an Indo-German Project

Matthias Pilz
Sarah Pierenkemper
and
David Meinhard

CONCEPT PUBLISHING COMPANY PVT., LTD.
NEW DELHI-110059

ISBN-13: 978-93-5125-023-4

First Published 2013

Published and Printed by

Concept Publishing Company Pvt. Ltd.
A/15-16, Commercial Block, Mohan Garden
New Delhi-110059 (India)
T: 25351460, 25351794, *F*: 091-11-25357109
E: publishing@conceptpub.com, W: www.conceptpub.com
Editorial Office: H-13, Bali Nagar, New Delhi-110 015, India.

Cataloging in Publication Data--*Courtesy:* D.K. Agencies (P) Ltd. <docinfo@dkagencies.com>

Pilz, Matthias.
Using the case method to support intercultural learning in higher education : findings from an Indo-German project / Matthias Pilz, Sarah Pierenkemper and David Meinhard.
p. cm.
Includes bibliographical references (p.).
ISBN 9789351250234

1. Education, Higher—Study and teaching—India—Methodology—Case studies. 2. Education, Higher—Study and teaching—Germany—Case studies. 3. Multiculturaleducation—India—Case studies. 4. Multicultural education Germany—Case studies. I. Pierenkemper, Sarah, joint author. II. Meinhard, David, joint author. III. Title.

DDC 378.54 23

Foreword

This volume is aimed at university teachers interested in teaching methodology in higher education. It also focuses on a pragmatic approach to teaching intercultural skills.

The introductory section sets out in detail the theoretical background to the development of the case study method in the context of research in teaching and learning. This is followed by a section on intercultural learning in universities, an area that is becoming increasingly important as teaching staff are required not simply to impart facts and knowledge but also to develop teaching methods that promote independent learning. The next section provides an overview of how case studies have developed as a teaching and learning arrangement and discusses the limitations on the applicability of the theory.

Three case studies are then reproduced as the basis for colleagues' own teaching. The authors would like to encourage readers to use these case studies in their own teaching and to adapt them to their own needs.

The final section provides comprehensive material on dealing with individual aspects of the case studies reproduced. These examples do not, of course, represent specimen answers; rather, they point to some possible interpretations and to the wide range of ways in which the material can be used. The documents also demonstrate how successful case studies can be in creating motivation, curiosity and creativity among students. A central requirement is that case studies are worked through by culturally diverse teams, since this is the only way in which discussion and comprehensive reflection on communication in a diverse cultural context will promote intercultural learning.

This project was carried out by the Center for Modern Indian Studies at the University of Cologne, which receives financial support from the German Academic Exchange Service (DAAD).

We would particularly like to thank the students who have been involved at the University of Cologne (Germany), the Vellore Institute of Technology (India) and the Tamil Nadu Agricultural University (India).

Our grateful thanks also to Kathrin Rasch and Christina Wilbertz from the University of Cologne for help with compiling the case studies and converting them into teaching and learning materials.

Contents

1

The Pedagogical Methodology of Case Studies and their Validity

The opportunities that case studies offer for learning and teaching have a long pedigree in university pedagogy (Copeland 1954). Case studies, case study methodology and working with case studies are not, therefore, recent phenomena but have long formed an integral part of university training in the field of economics (Pilz 2008); case studies illustrating practice from the world of business were, in fact, being used at Harvard Business School in Boston before the Second World War (Kaiser 1983, pp. 11f.). As theories of situational approaches are increasingly taken both to pedagogy and to curriculum design (Reetz 1984, p. 99-107 and 179-181), the case study as a tool for tackling complex issues through reallife manifestations gained popularity (Kaiser 1983, p. 16-20) and by the early 1970s, case studies had become an integral part of the methodology for teaching business studies (Pilz 1971, 1972, *inter alia*).

Since then, many different definitions and descriptions have been advanced for ‘Case Studies’, ‘Case Examples’ and ‘Case Methods’, all serving the diverse aims and aspirations of their authors. Here, we shall use the commonly adopted definition advanced by Reetz (1988a, p. 38), who defines case studies as “teaching materials in which real, or realistic, events from social life and particularly from business life are prepared as an example and then used as the basis for the development of teaching and learning materials” (authors’ own translation).

In the academic literature on case studies, authors frequently centre their discussions of their pedagogical uses on the ability of case studies to focus the study of complex economic issues on the collective search for decisions relating to the central question illustrated. Consequently, elements such as subject knowledge, methodological skills and social skills are involved (see, for example, Leenders/Maufette-Leenders/Erskine 2001, pp. 5-7; Pilz 1978, pp. 95-98; Kaiser/Kaminski 1994, p. 127). However, decisions are not directly tested in reality but form the subject of reflection against the backdrop of the circumstances represented by reality and, in many cases, compared with other approaches to solutions (see also Mauffette-Leenders/Erskine/Leenders 2005, p.4)

Despite the prime importance of the decision-making process, differing priorities apply to the learning outcomes associated with using case studies. For example, as students weigh up decisions and solutions, it may be particularly important for them to uncover the full range of problems or to gather information. The diverse intentions that underpin the pedagogical use of case studies in teaching have produced a distinction between various type of case studies, which Kaiser (1983, pp. 20-25) has systematised into a typology that is widely used (Fig. 1.1).

It can be stated that the learning process of all case study variants is oriented on a problematic situation and its solution. Following Kaiser (1983, pp. 25-29) this leads to a generally valid process structure, which allows different focal points (Fig. 1.2).

The concept of action-orientation developed from criticisms made of traditional business teaching, in particular the over-emphasis placed on pure transmission of information, the presentation of rigid and overladen structures of content that rely too heavily on legal content, unrealistic and simplistic material, teacher-centred teaching, and the mismatch between

Fig. 1.1: Variants of Case Studies

Method	Identifying the problem	Gathering information	Identifying alternative types of solution; solving the problem and adopting a decision	Critique of solutions
The Case Study Method	*Focus* The problems are not identified	Information is given	The information given is used to identify possible solutions to the problem and make decisions	Comparison of the solution identified with the real-life decision made
The Case Problem Method	Problems are explicitly identified	Information is given	*Focus* The problems identified and the information provided are used to identify possible solutions and make a decision	Possible comparison of the solution identified with the real-life decision made
The Case Incident Method	The case is presented only in part	*Focus* Participants must gather information themselves	Possible solutions are identified and the case is resolved	—
The Stated Problem Method	Problems are pre-existing and pre-defined	Information is given	Pre-existing solutions, including justifications, are provided; students may seek alternative solutions	*Focus* Critique of the solutions provided

Source: Slightly adapted from Kaiser 1983, p. 23.

Fig. 1.2: General Process Structure for Case Studies, following Kaiser	
1. *Confrontation*: Groups address the case study	*Aim*: Recognising the problem context and the decision-making context
2. *Information*: Groups survey the case material provided and identify their own sources of information	*Aim*: Learning to identify and evaluate the information needed to make a decision
3. *Exploration*: Each group discusses alternative solutions	*Aim*: Thinking of alternatives
4. *Resolution*: Each group makes its decision	*Aim*: Comparing and assessing possible solutions
5. *Disputation*: Each group defends its decision	*Aim*: Putting forward arguments to defend a decision
6. *Collation*: Groups compare their solution with the decision made in real life	*Aim*: Weighing up the benefits of individual solutions
Source: Kaiser 1983, p. 26.	

thought and action (*see*, for example, Kell/van Buer/Schneider 1992, pp. 521-524; Reetz 1984, pp. 23 35). Particular emphasis is placed on the use of multi-dimensional teaching and learning arrangements, such as game-playing, office and company simulations, 'junior companies', and case studies (for definitions and differentiations, see Achtenhagen 1997, pp. 623-632; Keim 1992) in the acquisition of key skills generally (Kaiser 1992; John 1992, pp. 85 and 89) and, more specifically, on the development of complex knowledge structures and their application and transformation in action situations (see, for example, Kaiser/Kaminski 1994, p. 115; John 1992; Preiß 1992). Both the construction and the transformation of knowledge are underpinned by cognitive networking processes, so teaching and learning arrangements are closely interlinked with networked thinking (Section 1). Experts in cognitive psychology as well as in business pedagogy recommend the use of such arrangements, including case studies, to promote networked thinking, since they represent a multi-dimensional and complex framework that forms the basis for the development and application of networked thinking (Preiß 1992; Reetz/Sievers 1983, pp. 93-97).

There are two reasons we have chosen case studies from the broad range of teaching and learning arrangements as a way of improving networked thinking. The first derives from the psychology of learning and relates to the fact that case studies, by being very strictly oriented to problem-solving, are by their nature particularly well suited to generating networked thinking structures; moreover, their mid-range realism is easier to adapt consistently to such an aim than other arrangements (John 1992, p. 84; Reetz 1988a, pp. 39-41; Reetz/Sievers 1983, pp. 98f.). Although the case study represents a less marked form of "learning modelling" (Achtenhagen *et al.* 1992, p. 128; Pilz 2002b) than other learning arrangements, this shortcoming is more than compensated for by students' knowledge that the action they take while learning (Achtenhagen *et al.* 1992, pp. 82-85) will have no real-life impact (Buddensiek 1992, p. 15) and by the scope for using the case study for the purposes of long-term reflection and subsequent evaluation.

The second reason relates more to the organisation of teaching and to the level of organisation and the time required for the exercise (Reetz 1992, pp. 345f.). For example, case studies impose no specific technical or space requirements of the kind that an office simulation does. Moreover, the 'single decision' they require makes it easier to plan and manage time than is the case, for example, with the 'revolving' decision-making processes involved in most gaming scenarios (Buddensiek 1992, p. 16) or with the disruption caused by suspending routine activities while running company or office simulations.

Against the backdrop of this review, we, therefore, now set out and justify the design principles for the case studies developed here for intercultural teaching within higher education. As John (1992, p. 85) warns, case studies cannot be assumed to be sure-fire successes, a warning to users about very careful design that is repeated by many other authors (Pilz *et al.* 2003).

Analysis of some of the key literature on this topic prompts us to formulate some 'rules', which we cite at length below (Fig. 1.3). However, it should be stressed that the list makes no claim to be exhaustive and that there may well be overlaps.

Fig. 1.3: Rules for Designing Case Studies

1. The learning outcomes relating to the case study must have been articulated and be the absolute priority in design terms.
2. Content must be free of contradictions and arranged logically, so that there is a clear path to learning.
3. Content must acknowledge the experiences and concepts learners have and their prior knowledge.
4. Content must be authentic and realistic.
5. The structure of the case must be problem-oriented and represent conflicts in the way it presents multiple contexts.
6. The structure of the case must be complex in terms of the elements presented.
7. The case must enable a number of different solutions to be found.
8. The description of the situation and, where appropriate, the documents and other sources of information provided must be comprehensive and tailored to the learning outcomes.
9. The case must motivate students to solve the problem.

Source: Authors' own compilation from Dubs 1996, pp. 164f.; Kaiser/Kaminski 1994, p. 142; Achtenhagen *et al.* 1992, pp. 74f.; Reetz 1988b.

We will now specify each of these 'rules' (see also Pilz *et al.*, 2003) in relation to the goal of providing training for economic behaviour in an intercultural context.

Economic behaviour in an intercultural context is a complex skill whose development in a practical context requires more than mere passive acquisition of elements of knowledge, such as principles learned by heart. The case study must always evoke learning situations that help learners consciously to tackle multidimensional linking elements. This can be achieved by appropriate trigger questions or tasks that also promote and support the learning process by pointing to complex problems (Stark *et al.*, 1995; Reetz 1988b, p. 153). Good examples here are the SWOT analysis and the decision matrix, tools that are commonly used in the teaching of management and that can be very helpful in presenting concretely the complexity and possible goal conflicts in relation to learners' justification for their decisions.

Although structured tasks clash with a purist view of the case study method, they can nonetheless help achieve rapid success and boost students' motivation in the long term, especially where a group of students includes varying levels of prior knowledge.

Moreover, learners should be challenged to articulate solid justificatory arguments when presenting the outcome of their consideration of a case study (Waibel 1996, p. 49). As discussion begins, any omissions are a positive element, because they can help deepen knowledge. And while the role of teachers is to act as moderators during the case study (Wolf 1992), this can be expanded during the initial phase and during the evaluation stage to include an "inductive learning discussion" (Dubs 1989, p. 52, authors' own translation) that actively steers learners' thinking processes and broadens them. In this context, cultural differences can then be illuminated from a different perspective and interpreted meaningfully.

Finally, it should be noted that the transfer of increased knowledge in terms of the skills required for economic action in an intercultural context to new and complex problem areas or content — especially in relation to real-life situations (Keim 1992, pp. 142f.) — will succeed only where university teaching offers "large volumes of transfer-oriented exercises" (Dubs 1989, p. 61, authors' own translation) and such exercises are not used merely as occasional departures from other teaching methods.

2

Selected Intercultural Aspects of Learning and Teaching

Globalisation and internationalisation, rapid technological development, tapping into and developing new markets — these are the long-term trends that are shaping our employment and economic lives in the twenty-first century. We inhabit a complex and rapidly changing environment that poses very specific challenges, so it is essential that educational and training establishments equip their students to tackle these challenges. Intercultural aspects are growing in importance to universities, and teachers are increasingly required to use more up-to-date teaching methods in which they themselves have not always received formal training (Palfreyman/McBride 2007, p. 1).

Against the backdrop of this evolving shift of focus from teaching to learning (see, for example, Barr/Tagg 1995), university students are increasingly viewed as active participants in the process of teaching and learning, while the importance of teacher-centred forms of teaching is declining. The promotion and encouragement of greater active involvement by students in the learning process, and the resultant increase in the level of student activity and collaborative forms of learning, increase the urgency of tackling diversity and cultural differences at the micro-level — that is, within individual teaching situations. The literature, however, identifies the absence of a cultural perspective in teaching and learning research: “The scholarship of content teaching and learning, therefore, remains without a serious attempt to view practice and research through a cultural lens across a range of contexts” (Palfreyman/McBride 2007, p. 2).

Nevertheless, learning and teaching in an intercultural context requires theoretical underpinning, for example, Hofstede's (1980) notion of general culture, which illustrates differences and relationships between individual national cultures by presenting them in terms of four dimensions: "power distance", "uncertainty avoidance", "individualism", and "masculinity". In a subsequent article, Hofstede represents a compressed version of his model and relates it explicitly to teaching and learning, seeking to explain the risk of misunderstanding between teacher and student by means of country-of-origin cultural differences (Hofstede 1986). In this context, Hofstede identifies a number of potential sources of "perplexities" (*ibid.*, p. 303) in the teaching and learning environment including cultural differences in the social status of the teachers and the students, differences in the extent to which the curriculum is perceived as 'relevant', differences in cognitive ability, and differences in the expected interaction between teachers and their students. Using a heuristic of the kind represented by Hofstede's proposed dimensions should not, of course, be allowed to produce over-simplistic and stereotypical perceptions among those involved in teaching and learning. Nevertheless, Hofstede argues that enhanced awareness of these cultural characteristics can be an asset in teaching: "Teaching to a student or student body with a cognitive ability profile different from what the teacher is accustomed to is evidently problematic; it demands a different didactic approach, for which the teacher may lack the proper cognitive abilities. At the same time, the surrounding environment usually reinforces people in their traditional cognitive ways and makes learning more difficult. There is no other solution to bridging this gap than increasing awareness, sustained effort on both sides, focusing on new abilities demanded by societal changes of the moment, and patience" (Hofstede 1986, p. 305).

Manikutty *et al.* (2007) establish a link between Hofstede's model and what are known as "approaches to learning"

(Marton/Säljö 1976) and draw specific and practical conclusions from it. In particular, they identify the risk of misunderstandings that may, for example, arise in academic exchange programmes involving German and Indian students when teachers are unaware of the cultural background and different approaches to learning manifested by students, which they then misinterpret (Manikutty *et al.* 2007, p. 86). They also point to the fact that knowledge of the target group's cultural origins and background could be an asset to a more target-group tailored teaching approach : "Teachers dealing with students from different cultures would benefit by understanding how the learning approaches of students from different cultures differ, and could deliver their courses with greater sensitivity to their diverse needs" (Manikutty *et al.* 2007, p. 85).

As we have already indicated, cultural characteristics are not just the preserve of students but apply also to teachers, who bring their own cultural background to their way of approaching interaction with students. (see also Erskine/Leenders/Maufette-Leenders 2003, pp. 211-214)". Jackson raises this issue and uses his perspective as a teacher to offer some pedagogical recommendations for how business case studies can be used effectively (Jackson 2008, pp. 81ff.). He also refers explicitly to the major challenge but also the enormous opportunities that business case studies represent for intercultural groups: "Teaching across cultures can be very rewarding but it also poses special challenges". Below, we present a number of examples taken from approaches to different groups.

This publication does not, however, specifically claim that it fills the gap we have identified in pedagogical theory. The aim is, rather, to present a report from practice to illustrate how case study-oriented teaching can be successful in a very heterogeneous target group. We also hope to remove the fear that many teachers feel when confronted with the method and that they will use the diverse cultural backgrounds of their own students as a shared opportunity for a successful shaping of the learning process.

3

Using Case Studies in Practical Higher Education Teaching

The Summer Schools run by the Centre for Modern Indian Studies at the University of Cologne in collaboration with two Indian universities trialled case studies as a learning method in an intercultural context. The case studies designed for the experiment were used in slightly modified form once each in one of the Indian universities and at the University of Cologne. Students worked on the material in groups that included both Indian and German students from different disciplines within economic and social sciences or management sciences.

The groups taking part were very heterogeneous, and the students had differing levels of prior knowledge and ability, something that was not assessed and reflected in group allocation. The focus of the work in designing the case study and overseeing its use by the students was, therefore, not the acquisition of specialist knowledge but the development and promotion of social skills, in particular intercultural skills as a specific form of social skill. The aim of the work on the case study was to use a realistic and complex problem to equip an intercultural group of students to acquire and enhance their intercultural skills by sharing knowledge and working together to devise solutions.

A key priority in designing the case study was devising a realistic setting with which both the Indian and the German students could identify. It was important that the case was designed in such a way that it was consonant with the perceptions and experience of all participants yet capable of stimulating intercultural discourse as a result of its problem orientation and the conflicts it threw up. The case study also had to be capable of being discussed and resolved within a very short timeframe (no more than two days) and without participants needing to gather additional data apart from information readily available online.

The case study was, therefore, designed to relate to the setting up of a German-Indian company, a scenario that would enable both German and Indian students to bring their own general and specialist knowledge to the case study work but that would not exclude students from other nationalities. Specific issues raised by national legislation, regulatory frameworks, work patterns and other characteristics, as well as additional difficulties, were discussed within the group, raising awareness and understanding of other cultures.

The task brief was to draw up a detailed business plan that included all relevant operational resources, procedures and processes. The students were referred to existing online guidance on drawing up business plans to help them (http://www.entrepreneur.com/article/38290, last accessed 15.08.2012). This relatively marked structuring of the stages they were expected to go through and the eventual outcome were influenced by two factors: the time constraint on the task and the fact that the students had very different levels of prior knowledge. The students presented their findings to staff and students at the relevant university, each presentation lasting around 30 minutes. Although the groups had a free choice in how they presented their decisions, all of them opted to use Power Point to support their presentation. After each group's presentation, its findings were discussed in the large group setting and participants were encouraged to reflect in depth on their experiences of intercultural team-working.

4
Teaching and Learning Materials

The rest of this volume is devoted to three case studies made available for use in university teaching. It goes without saying that before these case studies can be used, they need to be adapted to the prior knowledge and needs of the students for whom they are intended. Of central importance alongside the specialist knowledge aspect is the fact that implementation of problem-rich briefs and/or time constraints encouraged the student teams to communicate with each other and, where problems arose, to resolve them. Two crucial factors emerged here. First, it is essential that the teams always include members from differing cultural backgrounds and second, the reflection on communication processes is vital. The teacher should be assuming the role of moderator, for example encouraging students to reflect on and interpret cultural differences during group discussions. Other university teaching methods may also be useful in addition to the process of reflection, such as observation and subsequent evaluation (where did problems arise in intercultural communication and why?) or the subsequent role-playing of team processes.

With a view to developing intercultural skills in the long term, case studies may also, of course, be embedded in a longer-term learning process comprising further elements of intercultural learning, such as interviewing experts from other cultures or visiting another country.

Finally, we would point out that the detailed technical compilation of case studies relies on the availability of additional material. Teachers need to make appropriate textbooks and other sources of information available on the basis of the students' prior knowledge. Alternatively, or also, advanced students may make intensive use of online resources, for example to research import regulations, tariffs, taxation rates, market research, types of company, or production and transport costs.

WORKING GROUP A : GARAM MASALA

Introduction

During a Summer School you decide to offer the German students a very special treat while preparing an original Indian vegetable curry. Luckily you brought some homemade *garam masala* along from India.

After tasting a German boy claims: "Amazing, although I have been to many Indian restaurants in Germany so far, the taste of the meal is incomparable to the Indian dishes I tried before. There is nothing you can compare to this full, strong and spicy flavour". "Yes, the food tastes amazing, not like anything I tried so far. What is it that makes the taste so unique"? another German student asks. You tell them that it is a special mixture from your old grand-aunt which she sells at a small corner shop at a village next to Chennai.

What happens next?

You cannot stop thinking about how much the German students liked your vegetable curry.

After a restless night you are meeting with some of your fellow students to discuss the chances of success in selling *garam masala* and other Indian spices in selected stores/places in Germany. As time passes by, your ideas begin to take concrete form until one student in your group claims, "Let's set up our own business"!

The next day, the suggestion to start an own business is still tempting. Unfortunately, you and your fellow students cannot provide enough equity capital for the foundation of your start-up venture.

However, to ensure a good start for your company, you need more money. At the local Entrepreneurs Trade fair you get the chance to introduce your idea to potential investors.

Time is short now. The Trade Fair Board has told you to present a comprehensive idea of your future business with the help of a *business plan*.

Work Assignment

Now, it is your task to develop and present a business plan for the production and export of Indian spices to Germany to potential investors at a meeting.

For a start, you will find some general information on how to write a *business plan* attached. In a next step, you and your fellow students may have to gather more information. For this purpose, there will be laptops with internet access available.

Your explanation should include all important informations required for setting up of business and must not be longer than 30 minutes. It is left to your decision which media you choose for presenting your business plan.

Information: It is recommended to use a template of a business plan as available on the Internet at: http://www.entrepreneur.com/article/38290.

WORKING GROUP B : CLOTHING

Introduction

During a Summer School one night you sit together with some German students. The German students are very interested in your life back in India. So you show them some pictures of your family and friends.

Especially the German girls are fascinated about the clothes the Indian girls are wearing. “Beautiful, these colourful robes and dresses you and your friends are wearing, are they traditional clothes?” a German girl asks. You tell them, that they are called *salwar kameez* and that rural Indian women embroider the ornaments by hand. “My mum works in a small fashion shop on one of the most expensive shopping promenades in Cologne” another girl comments on the conversation. “Mostly she has wealthy customers who always want to have something very special. I bet they would pay a lot of money for such unique cloth.

What happens next?

You cannot stop thinking about the conversation. After a restless night you are meeting with some of your fellow students to discuss the chances of success in selling Indian robes in selected stores/places in Germany. As time passes by, your ideas begin to take concrete form until one student in your group claims “Let’s set up our own business”!

On the next day, the suggestion to start an own business is still tempting. Unfortunately, you and your fellow students cannot provide enough equity capital for the foundation of your start-up venture.

However, to ensure a good start for your company, you need more money. At the local Entrepreneurs Trade Fair you get the chance to introduce your idea to potential investors.

Time is short now. The Trade Fair board has told you to present a comprehensive idea of your future business with the help of a *business plan*.

Work Assignment

Now, it is your task to develop and present a business plan for the production and export of *salwar kameez* to Germany to potential investors at a meeting.

For a start, you will find some general information on how to write a *business plan* attached. In a next step, you and your fellow students may have to gather more information. For this purpose, there will be laptops with internet access available.

Your explanation should include all important information required for setting up of business and must not be longer than 30 minutes. It is left to your decision which media you choose for presenting your business plan.

Information: It is recommended to use a template of a business plan as available on the Internet at: http://www.entrepreneur.com/article/38290.

WORKING GROUP C : *ORNAMENTS*

Introduction

During a Summer School, all the German girls are so fascinated by the beautiful golden ornaments you and all the other Indian girls are wearing. One of them says: "Wow ! The jewellery you are wearing look amazing, just exactly like the pieces they wear in the Bollywood movies, I bet they cost a fortune". "No, not at all", you answer. "These pieces for example, I bought at a small market in a village close to Chennai. They just cost some rupees." A German boy exclaims: "I am sure a lot of German teenagers would love Indian jewellery".

What happens next?

You cannot stop thinking about how the German students liked your beautiful golden ornaments. After a restless night you are meeting with some of your fellow students to discuss the chances of success in selling Indian ornaments and jewellery in selected stores/places in Germany. As time passes by, your ideas begin to take concrete form until one student in your group exclaims, "Let's set up our own business"!

On the next day, the suggestion to start an own business is still tempting. Unfortunately, you and your fellow students cannot provide enough equity capital for the foundation of your start-up venture.

However, to ensure a good start for your company, you need more money. At the local Entrepreneurs Trade Fair you get the chance to introduce your idea to potential investors.

Time is short now. The Trade Fair Board has told you to present a comprehensive idea of your future business with the help of a *business plan*.

Work Assignment

Now, it is your task to develop and present a business plan for the production and export of artificial Indian ornaments to Germany to potential investors at a meeting.

For a start, you will find some general information on how to write a *business plan* attached. In a next step, you and your fellow students may have to gather more informations. For this purpose, there will be laptops with internet access available.

Your explanation should include all important information required for setting up of business and must not be longer than 30 minutes. It is left to your decision which media you choose for presenting your business plan.

Information: It is recommended to use a template of a business plan as available on the Internet at: http://www.entrepreneur.com/article/38290.

5
Exemplary Results

Below, we present a number of extracts from the approaches devised by various groups to serve as examples. These examples are not, however, models: it is important to remember that the case study is designed to be open, so that differing solutions are possible. Assessing their technical accuracy should be a separate process.

Students were given a free hand in the method of presentation, but the groups all chose to use Power Point to support their presentation.

In general, it can be seen that all groups reached relevant conclusions within the time allowed, suggesting that the case study was set at an appropriate level of difficulty. It was also very evident from the presentations that the students had engaged in depth with the material. They defended their ideas eloquently and self-confidently in the subsequent discussion, and it became clear that the students had succeeded in thinking themselves into the constructed learning situation, which points also to a high level of case study authenticity. A very high level of motivation was also observable in those taking part in the case study, which was clearly linked to the teaching and learning methodology chosen. In short, the effects we observed reflected what we expected from the pedagogical theory set out above in relation to case studies.

Analysis of the content of the solutions identified shows that the students had applied management theory tools to solve the problems raised by the case study (for example a SWOT analysis to assess competition in a specific market or market segment) even though the task brief did not explicitly require them to do so. This may be seen as evidence that the case study as presented was being used as a learning environment that promotes the transfer of knowledge and that, in contrast to the acquisition and reproduction of static knowledge, the students had succeeded in applying general theories and tools to a specific task.

Observations of students' learning and working processes led to the conclusion that collaboration within intercultural teams had taken place without major disagreements, and that despite their cultural differences, the students had generally worked well together and complemented one other. Student feedback on the exercise was also very positive. We would explicitly reiterate here that reflecting on communications processes and revealing and explaining the reasons for successful cooperation, as well as for problems and misunderstandings in the teams, is the main concern in the context of intercultural learning.

We conclude that choosing the case study method as a way of organising teaching and learning in higher education proved very fruitful in this specific context and will be repeated if possible. Any teacher who is interested is actively encouraged to experiment with the case method in other settings and cultural environments and to make his or her findings and experiences accessible for colleagues to use in their own practice.

WORKING GROUP A *'GARAM MASALA'*

Vision

- to improve Per capita consumption of spices in Germany from 752 grams to 852 grams.

Mission

- to increase consumption of our products among all strata of people in Germany.
- to expand our business throughout the country

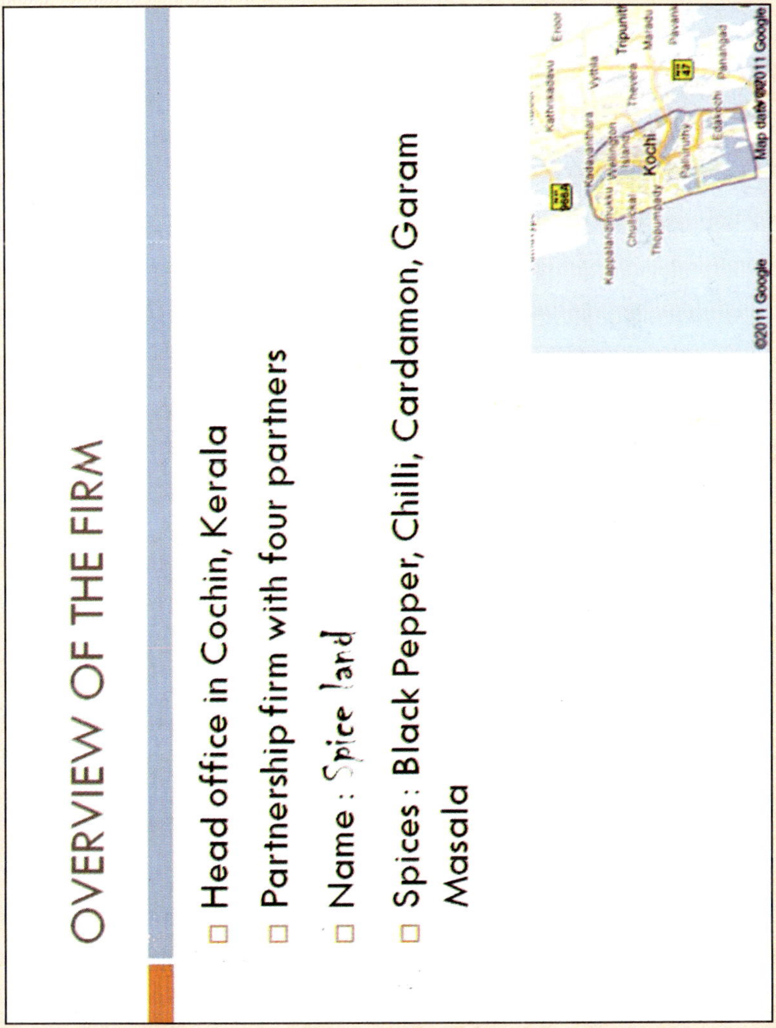
OVERVIEW OF THE FIRM
Head office in Cochin, Kerala
Partnership firm with four partners
Name : Spice land
Spices : Black Pepper, Chilli, Cardamon, Garam Masala
Kochi
©2011 Google

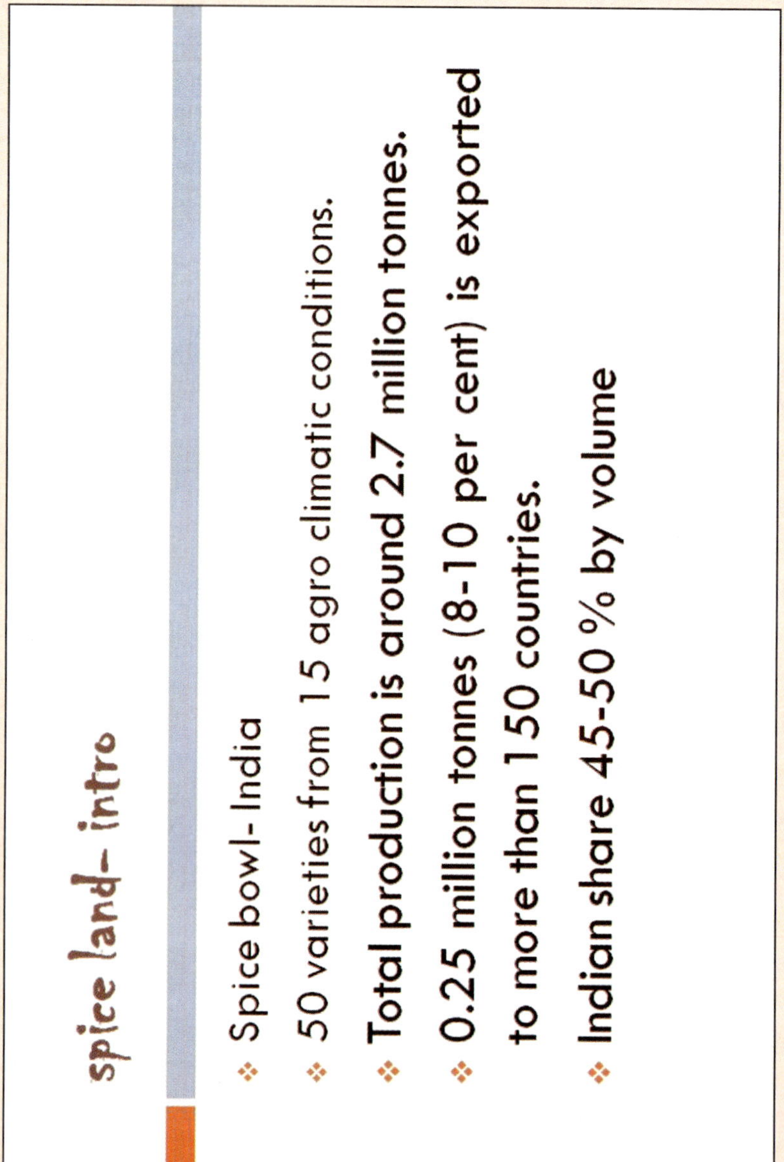
spice land- intro
Spice bowl- India
50 varieties from 15 agro climatic conditions.
Total production is around 2.7 million tonnes.
0.25 million tonnes (8-10 per cent) is exported to more than 150 countries.
Indian share 45-50% by volume

PRODUCT- Export basket

- Whole spices - 43
- Spice mixes - 4
- Blends - 8
- Curry Powders / Mixtures - 18
- Oleoresins - 30
- Essential oils - 38
- De-hydrated spice - 3
- Freeze dried spice
- Spice in brine
- Other value added products - 4

Organic spices – Ecocert international,germany

Quantities : 100, 200 & 250 grams for retailers
1kg for commercial purpose.

❖European Spice Association (ESA)

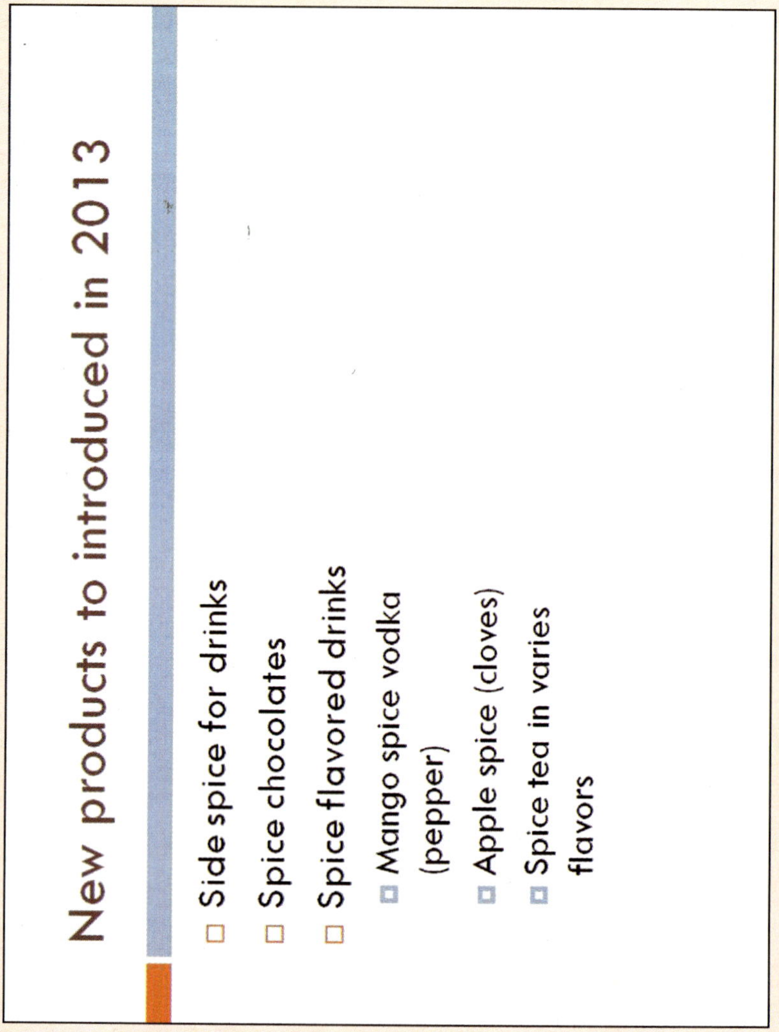
New products to introduced in 2013
Side spice for drinks
Spice chocolates
Spice flavored drinks
Mango spice vodka (pepper)
Apple spice (cloves)
Spice tea in varies flavors

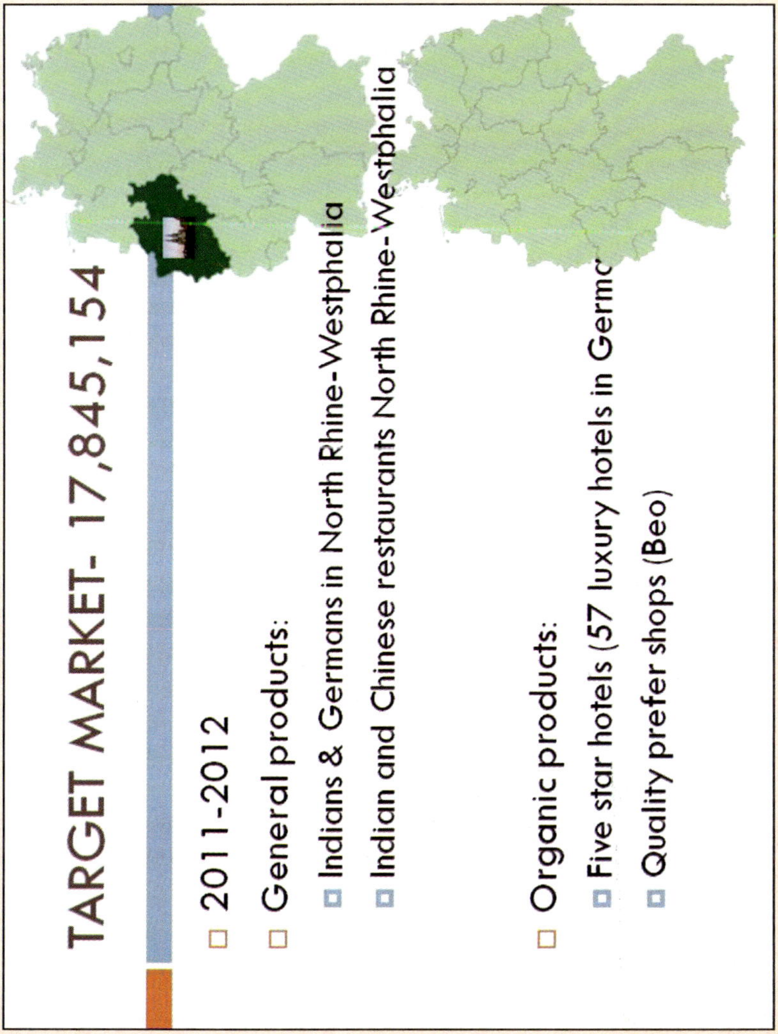
TARGET MARKET- 17,845,154
2011-2012
General products:
Indians & Germans in North Rhine-Westphalia
Indian and Chinese restaurants North Rhine-Westphalia
Organic products:
Five star hotels (57 luxury hotels in Germ
Quality prefer shops (Beo)

TARGET MARKET Phase II- 3,440,441

- 2013-2014 Ordinary products:
  - Indians & Germans in Berlin
  - Indian and Chinese restaurants Berlin

Metro & Cities – also be covered from 2015 onwards.

Sale of spices in Germany

Country	2006-07 In crore	2007-08 in crore	%change in 2007-08 over 2006-07
Germany	216.09	217.26	0.54

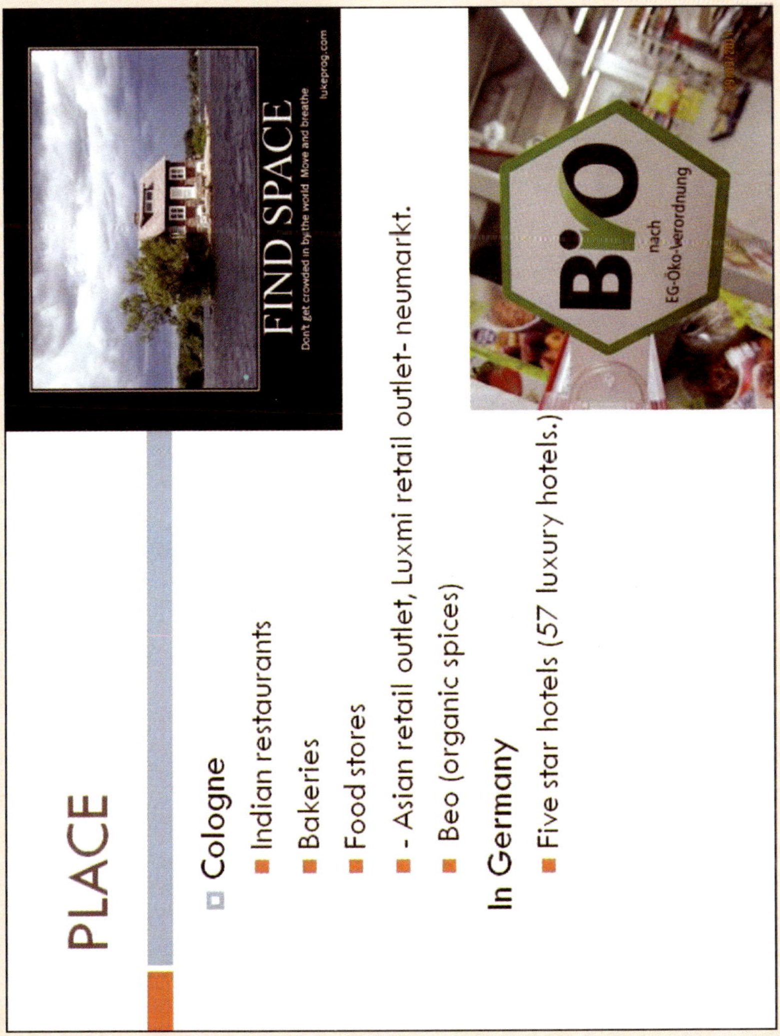
PLACE
Cologne
Indian restaurants
Bakeries
Food stores
- Asian retail outlet, Luxmi retail outlet- neumarkt.
Beo (organic spices)
In Germany
Five star hotels (57 luxury hotels.)
FIND SPACE
Don't get crowded in by the world Move and breathe
lukeprog.com
Bio
nach
EG-Öko-Verordnung

Price in Euro's

Package :

100 gram – 1.26

200 gram – 2.53

250 gram – 2.96

1 kg – 15.0 (10% extra)

Price Discounts

- Quantity discount
- Cumulative quantity discount
- Seasonal discount
- Trade discount

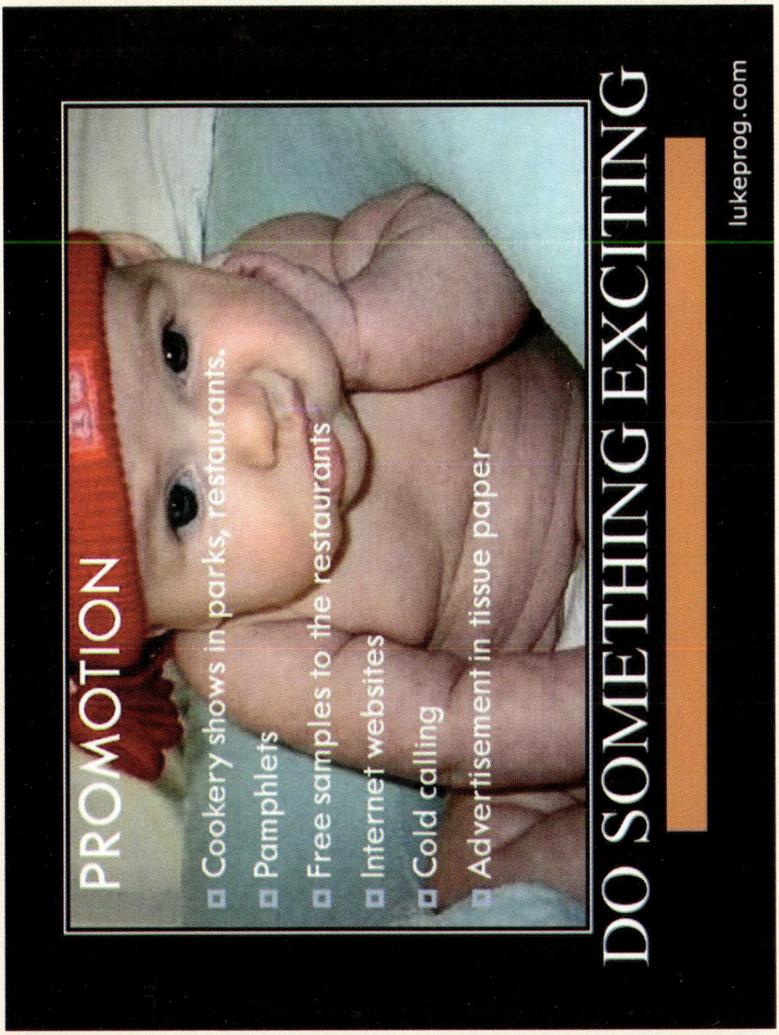
PROMOTION
Cookery shows in parks, restaurants.
Pamphlets
Free samples to the restaurants
Internet websites
Cold calling
Advertisement in tissue paper
DO SOMETHING EXCITING
lukeprog.com

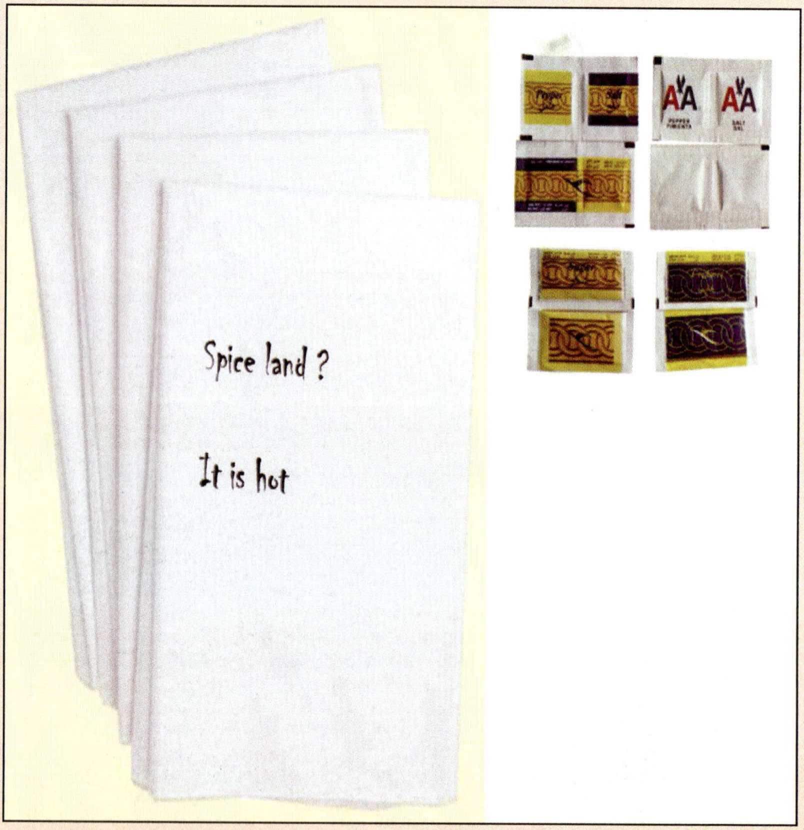
Spice land ?
It is hot

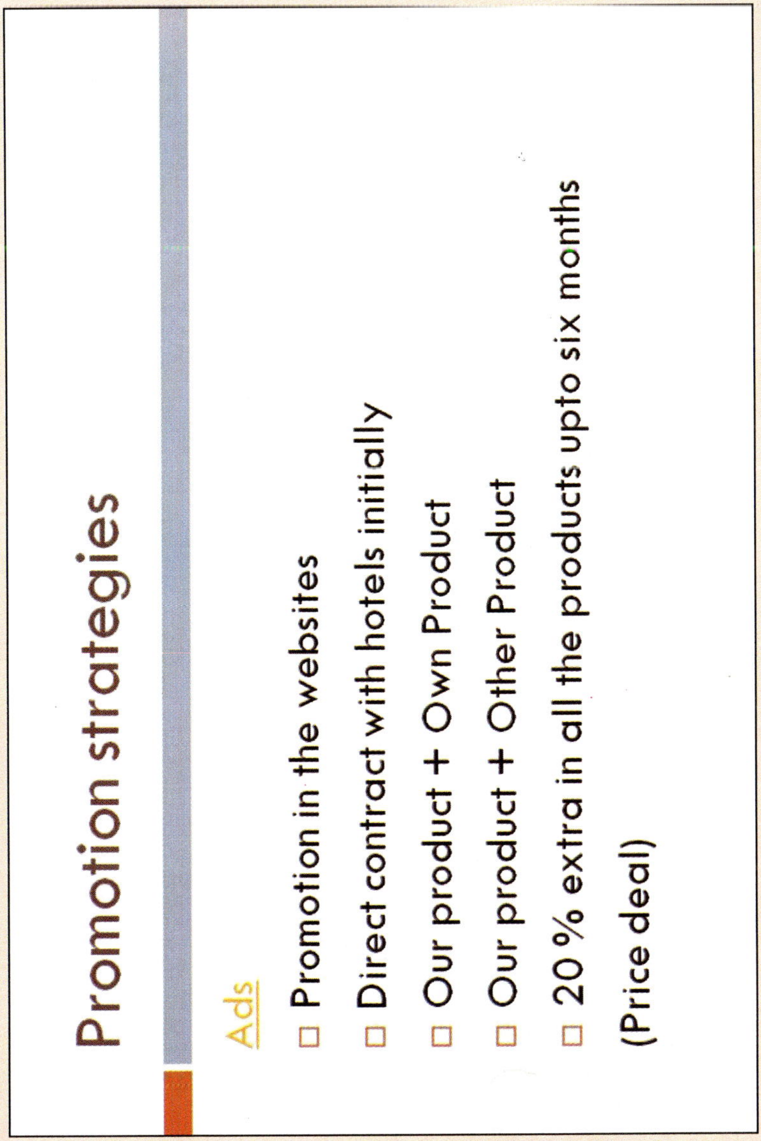
Promotion strategies
Ads
Promotion in the websites
Direct contract with hotels initially
Our product + Own Product
Our product + Other Product
20 % extra in all the products upto six months
(Price deal)

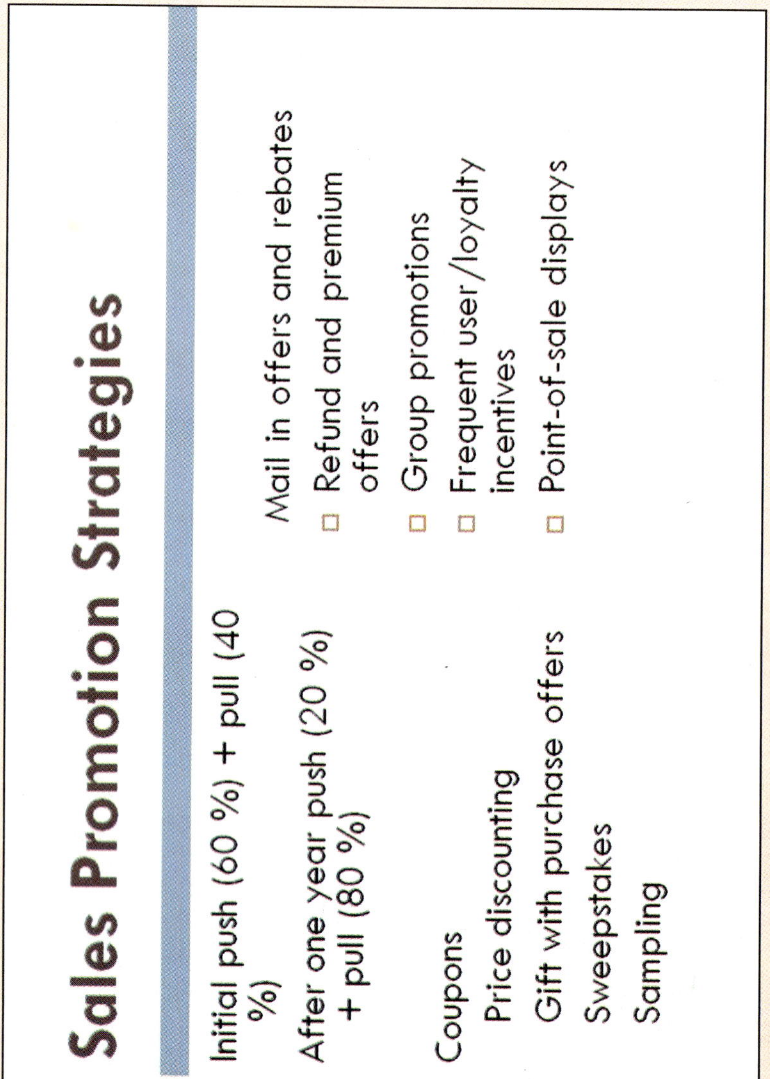
Sales Promotion Strategies
Initial push (60 %) + pull (40 %)
After one year push (20 %) + pull (80 %)
Coupons
Price discounting
Gift with purchase offers
Sweepstakes
Sampling
Mail in offers and rebates
Refund and premium offers
Group promotions
Frequent user/loyalty incentives
Point-of-sale displays

Spiceland2u.com
Spice land
All cities can access
this service
Service at your
doorstep within one
hour
ONLINE PURCHASE
Product Range
Whole spices
Grounded spices
Turmeric Powder
Chilly Powder
Crushed Chilly
Coriander Powder
Black Pepper Powder
Curry Powder
Tamarind
Grains and Pulses
Oil seeds

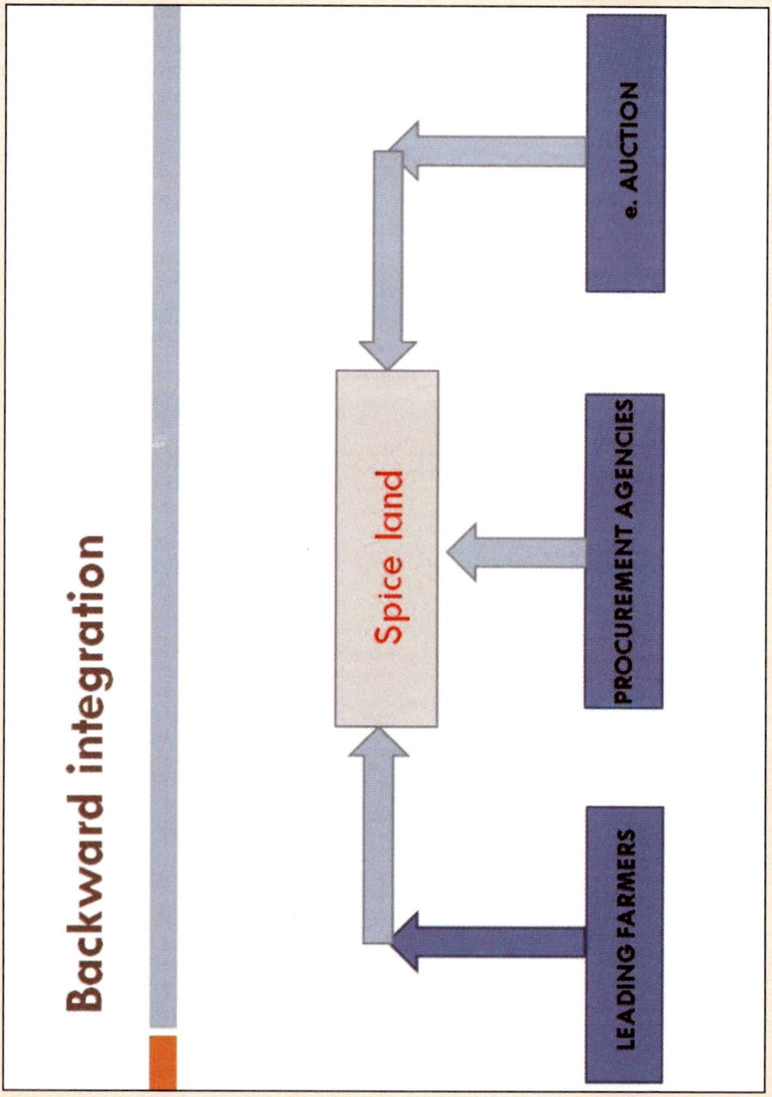
Backward integration
Spice land
e. AUCTION
PROCUREMENT AGENCIES
LEADING FARMERS

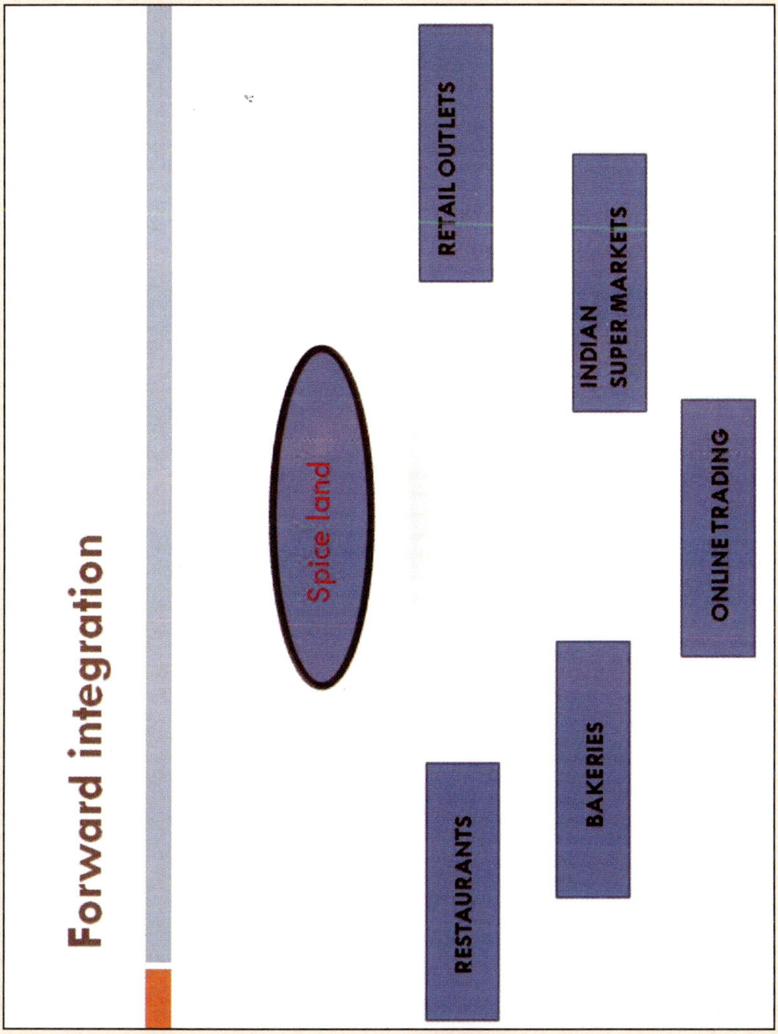
Forward integration
Spice land
RETAIL OUTLETS
INDIAN
SUPER MARKETS
ONLINE TRADING
BAKERIES
RESTAURANTS

COMPETITORS
TRS- 40
SHAN- 40
MDH- 22
AACHI- 10
GRANDMA- 10
PASCO
CLOVES
2.59

Quality standards

Name of Country/Spice	Extraneous matter %/wt.	Moisture %/wt.	Total ash /%wt.	Acid insoluble ash %/wt.
Germany				
Chilli	---	10	8	1
Celery	---	10	12	2.5
Coriander	---	---	8	2.5
Dill	---	12.5	7	1
Fennel	---	10	10	1
Fenugreek	---	10	5	1
Ginger	---	12.5	7	1
Pepper	---	12	7	1
Turmeric	---	10	7	1.5

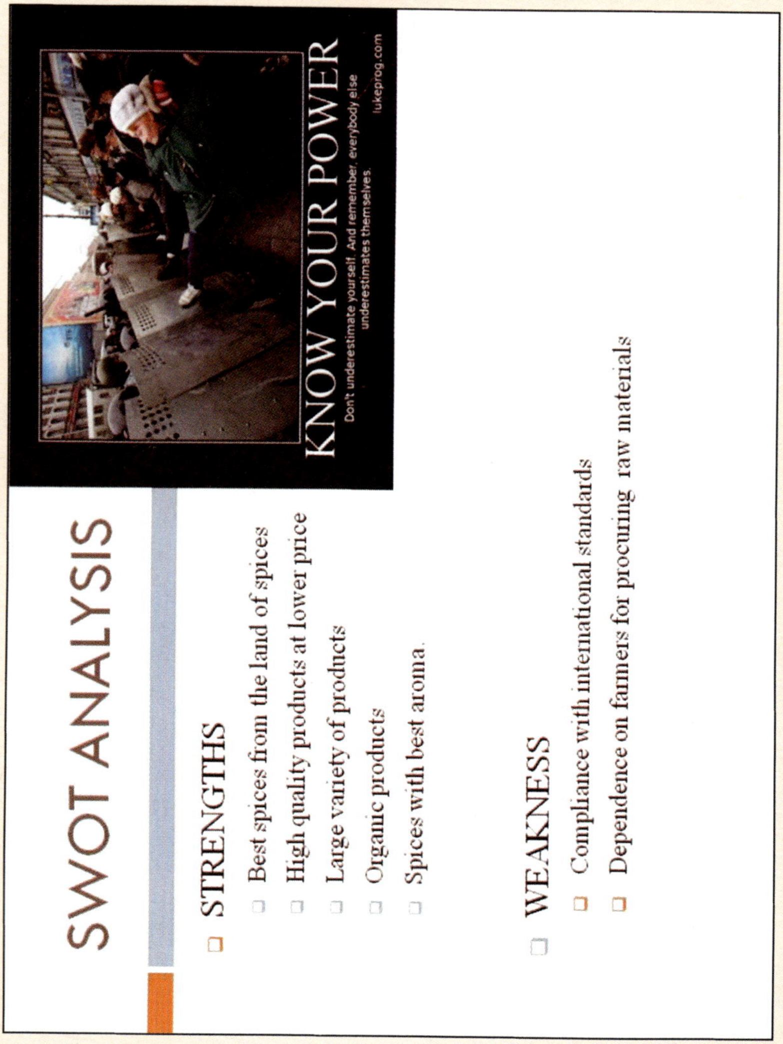
SWOT ANALYSIS
STRENGTHS
Best spices from the land of spices
High quality products at lower price
Large variety of products
Organic products
Spices with best aroma.
WEAKNESS
Compliance with international standards
Dependence on farmers for procuring raw materials
KNOW YOUR POWER
Don't underestimate yourself. And remember, everybody else underestimates themselves.
lukeprog.com

Conti…

- OPPORTUNITIES
  - Wide scope of spice market in Germany
  - Presence of Indian restaurants
  - Product specialization and differentiation
  - Increased usage of organic products

- Threats
  - Competitors
  - Non acceptance of the product by the target customers
  - Probability of imitation

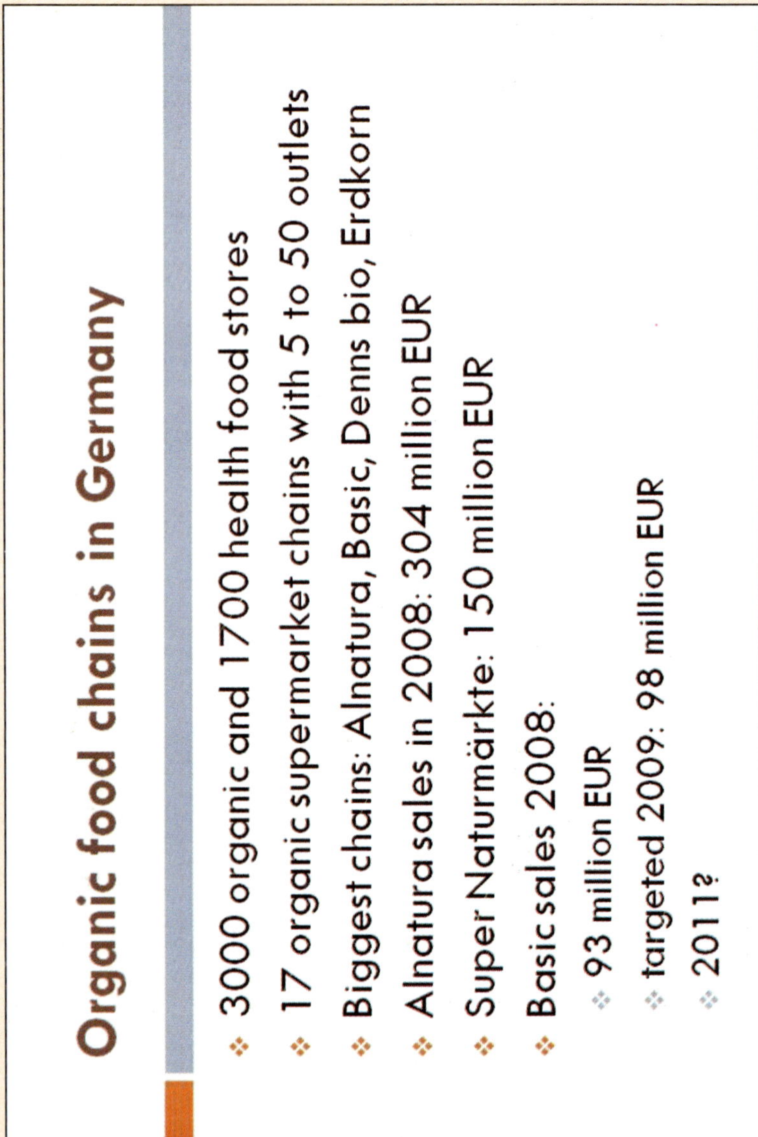
Organic food chains in Germany
3000 organic and 1700 health food stores
17 organic supermarket chains with 5 to 50 outlets
Biggest chains: Alnatura, Basic, Denns bio, Erdkorn
Alnatura sales in 2008: 304 million EUR
Super Naturmärkte: 150 million EUR
Basic sales 2008:
93 million EUR
targeted 2009: 98 million EUR
2011?

Spice board

- 50% -Rs.25.00 lakhs -product R&D.
- Patent - upto Rs.1.00 crore.

Promotion of Indian Spice Brands Abroad

Product and Packaging Development and Bar Coding

Brand Promotion.

- Interest free loan upto 100% for slotting/listing fee, Promotional measures
- Product development- Rs.2.50 crores per brand
- Rs.5.00 crores for buyout.

International Trade Fairs/Meetings

1. Participation in International fairs/exhibitions
2. Participation in International meetings/seminars is assisted for market expansion.

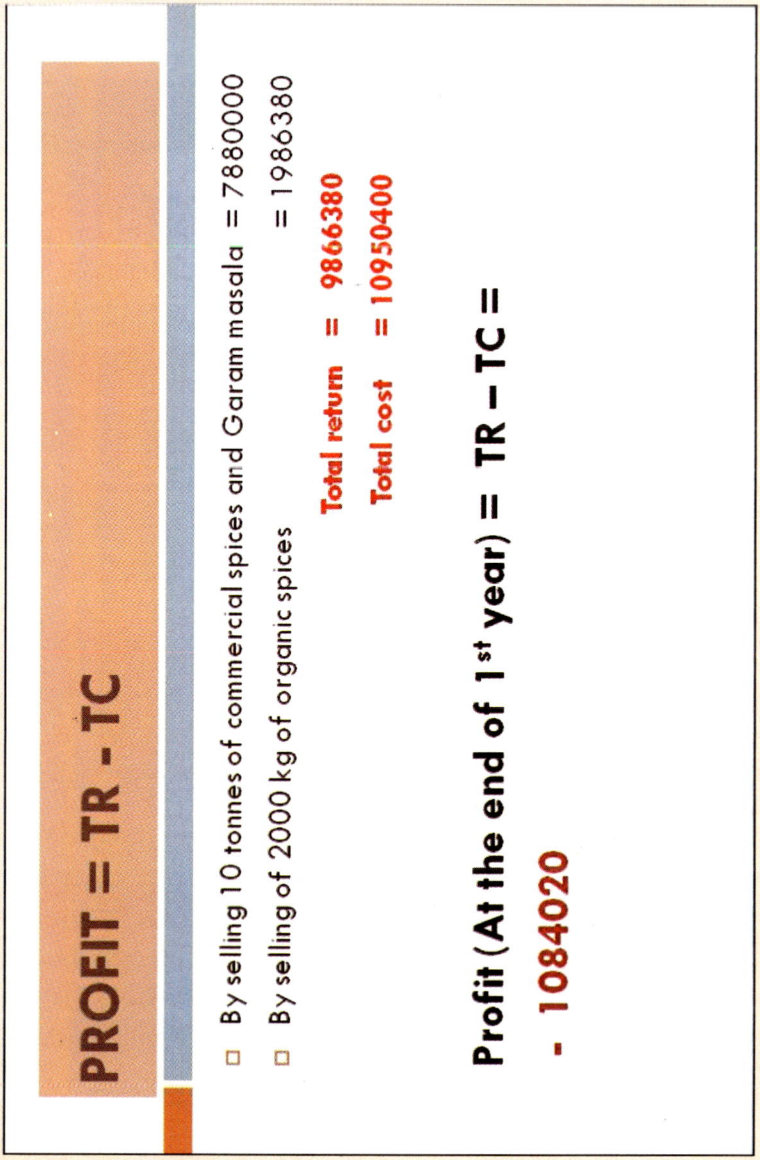
PROFIT = TR - TC
By selling 10 tonnes of commercial spices and Garam masala = 7880000
By selling of 2000 kg of organic spices = 1986380
Total return = 9866380
Total cost = 10950400
Profit (At the end of 1st year) = TR – TC =
- 1084020

WORKING GROUP B *'CLOTHING'*

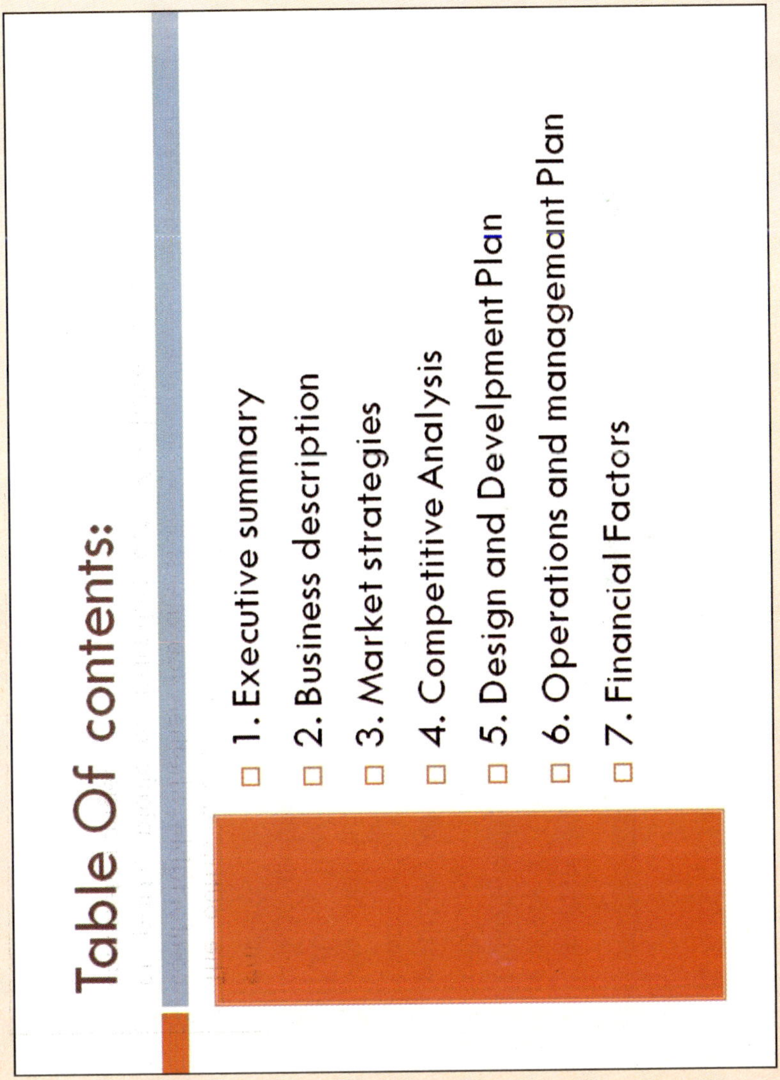
Table Of contents:
1. Executive summary
2. Business description
3. Market strategies
4. Competitive Analysis
5. Design and Develpment Plan
6. Operations and managemant Plan
7. Financial Factors

Executive Summary

- 'Namaste India' is a exporter of Indian Garments. We deal in a wide variety of Garments mainly concentrated on Salwar Kameez catering to customers design tastes and preferences.
- With our contemporary range of Salwar Kameez one can feel positively effervescent when they wear them and it will surely add glamour to their personality.
- We shall have eye catching combination of embroidery on the rich fabric. These colourful and stunning patterns make the collection of chikan embroidered kurtis a definite stunner and the variety being endless.
- The outfits are made of fine fabric to make you relax and feel comfortable whether you are staying at home or going to the office or party, picnic or partying out. We have a very different and complete range.

Namaste INDIA

- We offer Salwar Kameez that come from Indian states of Punjab, Uttar Pradesh.
- The very common and comfortable outfit from India is nowdays popular in other countries too.
- We can very easily find women wearing Salwar Kameez in different continents.
- Salwar Kameez is available in many designs like short kurties and churidaar pajamis, long kurties with salwar etc.

- **Who are we ?**
- We design, retail, wholesale, manufacture export women fashion apparels. Its old meets new, east meets west, traditional meets contemporary. Most of these outfits are designed and manufactured in-house, the rest are exclusively commissioned from craftsmen & weavers across India.
- **What we are not -**
- We are not an IT company depending on 3rd or 4th parties for their supply and customer service and problem of not having product knowledge. We are not a gifting company dealing in cakes / flowers and other unrelated products. We just specialize in salwar kameez as we eat, drink and sleep women fashion. For us your ordered outfit is more than just SKU or some alpha numeric code

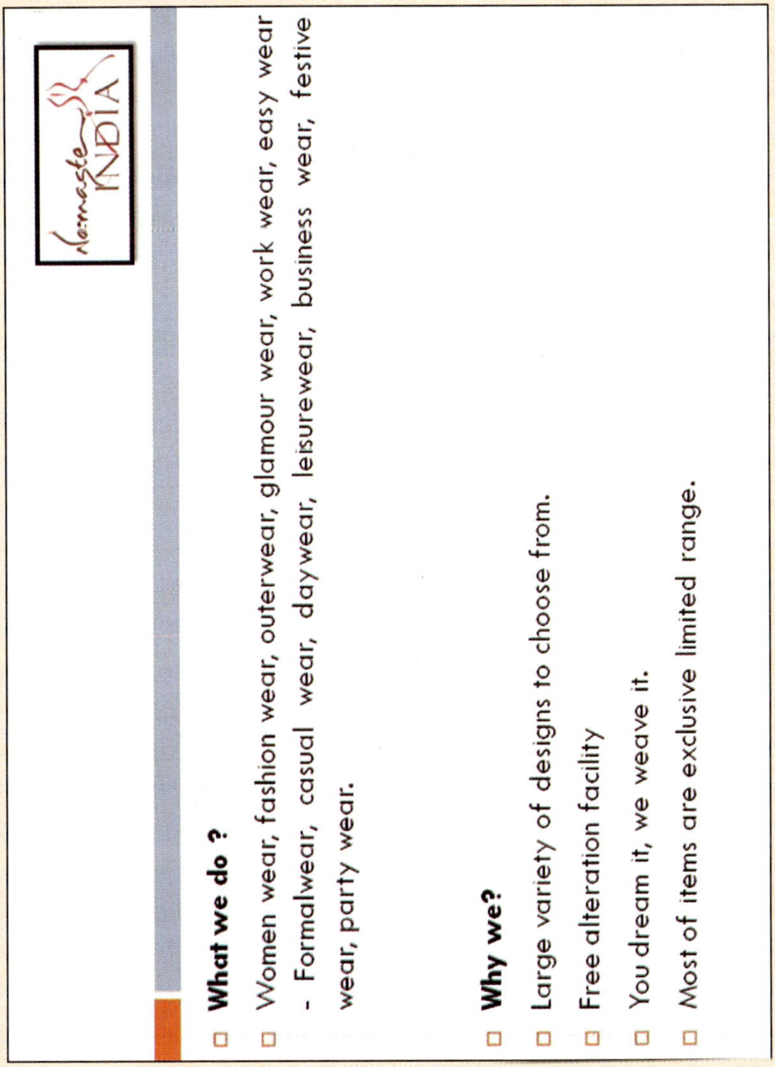
Namaste INDIA
What we do ?
Women wear, fashion wear, outerwear, glamour wear, work wear, easy wear - Formalwear, casual wear, daywear, leisurewear, business wear, festive wear, party wear.
Why we?
Large variety of designs to choose from.
Free alteration facility
You dream it, we weave it.
Most of items are exclusive limited range.

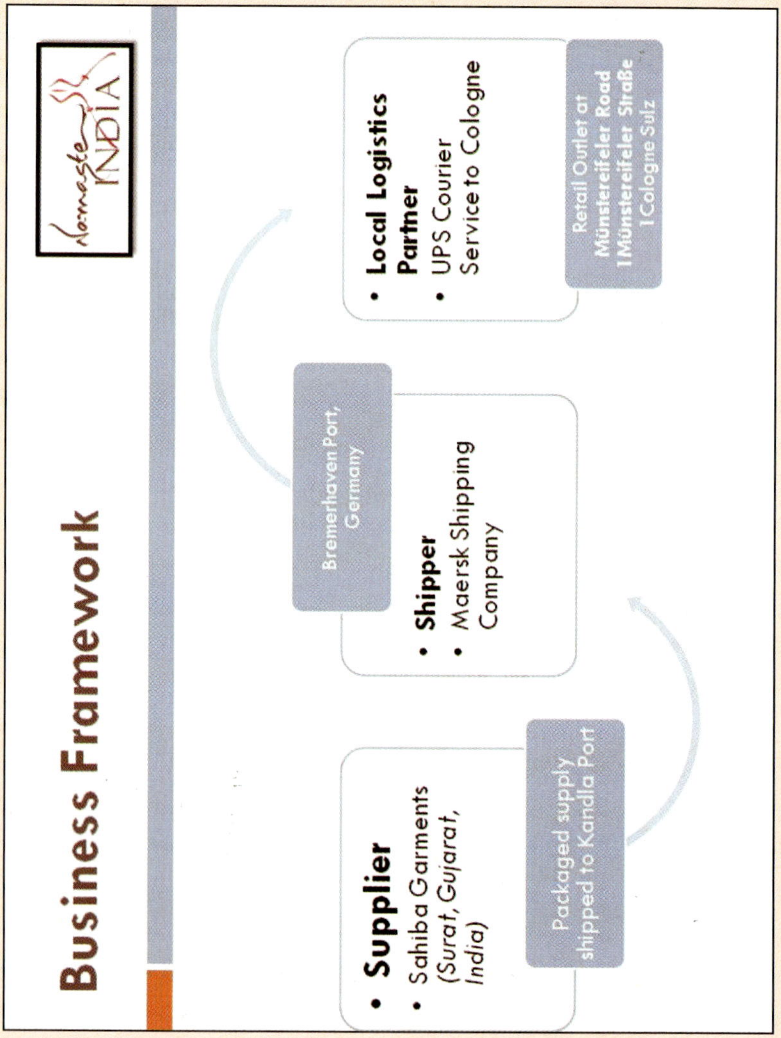
Business Framework
Namaste INDIA
Supplier
Sahiba Garments (Surat, Gujarat, India)
Packaged supply shipped to Kandla Port
Shipper
Maersk Shipping Company
Bremerhaven Port, Germany
Local Logistics Partner
UPS Courier Service to Cologne
Retail Outlet at Münstereifeler Road 1 Münstereifeler Straße 1 Cologne Sulz

Germany: Market for Garment Exports from India

- Germany has long been the bellwether of fashion and accessories market ahead Britain, Italy, France and other Europe countries, accounting for an overwhelming annual retail sales of EUR$55 billion. *(Source: APEC Report of Asia Apparel fair 2012)*
- The ever-increasing demand for high quality but competitively priced Asian garment products by Europe market is offering all Asian suppliers ample business expansion opportunities
- Exports of garments and other textile items from India to Germany in the Year 2009-10 was Rs. 1542 millions. *(Source: Ministry of Textile, Govt. of India)*

SWOT Analysis:

Strengths:

- Availability of quality supply of product
- Unique selling proposition in cologne
- Strong supplier relation
- Strong entry barrier

Weakness:

- Uncertain demand conditions
- No of stores opened is limited to one.
- Acceptance in unknown

SWOT Analysis

Namaste INDIA

Opportunities:

- Relatively untapped market
- Opportunities to expand the product line and enter new segments and new stores
- Cultural advantages
- Low no of players in this segment

Threats:

- New entrants
- Climatic conditions prevalent in Cologne
- Legal and regulatory framework
- Currency rate fluctuations

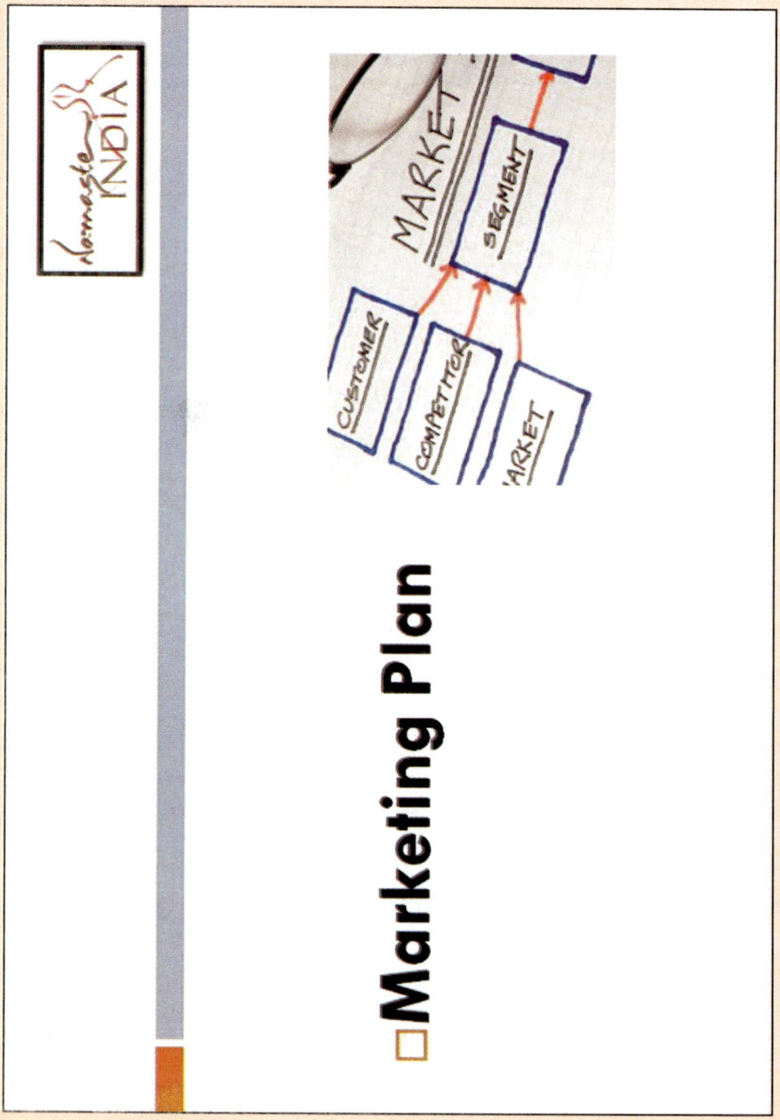
Namaste INDIA
Marketing Plan
MARKET
SEGMENT
CUSTOMER
COMPETITOR

Marketing Strategy

- A delighted customer is our best brand ambassador
- USP: quality of the fabric and the cultivated image of 'Indianess'
- Key elements: word of mouth publicity, leaflets, direct mails.

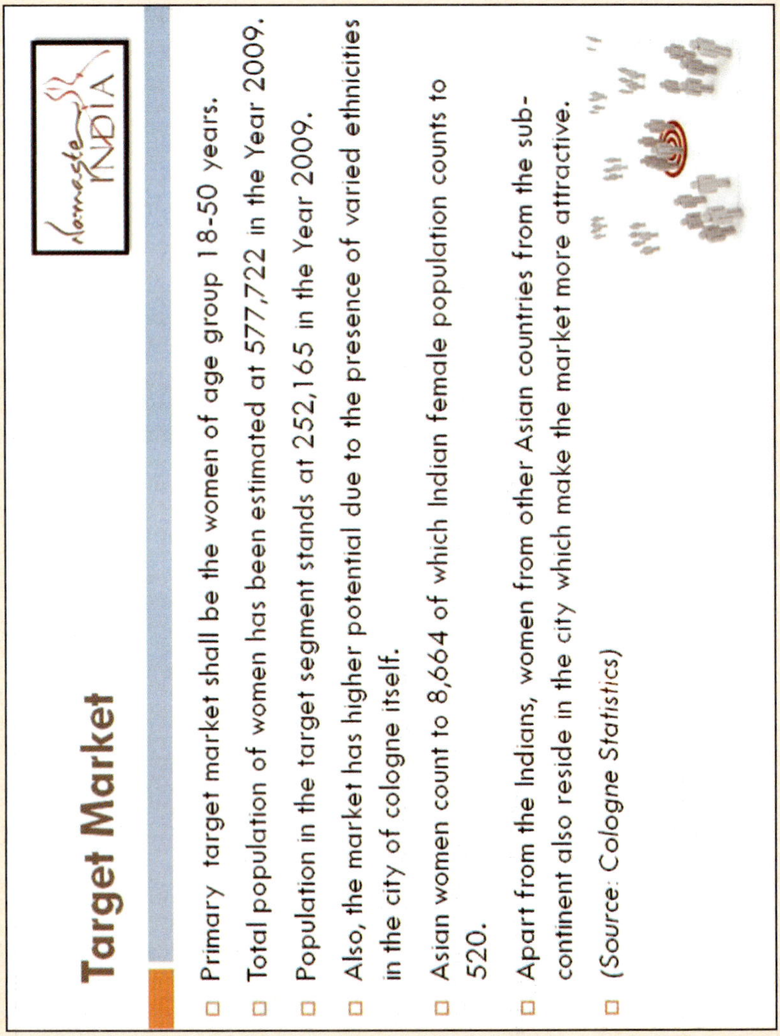
Target Market
Namaste INDIA
Primary target market shall be the women of age group 18-50 years.
Total population of women has been estimated at 577,722 in the Year 2009.
Population in the target segment stands at 252,165 in the Year 2009.
Also, the market has higher potential due to the presence of varied ethnicities in the city of cologne itself.
Asian women count to 8,664 of which Indian female population counts to 520.
Apart from the Indians, women from other Asian countries from the sub-continent also reside in the city which make the market more attractive.
(Source: Cologne Statistics)

Namaste INDIA

Product:

- Salwar Kameez are traditional Indian outfits that have been gaining popularity over the years. They are both ethnic Indian wear as well are trendy to suit the taste and preferences of the women in Germany. Vibrant and bright colors will definitely attract the attention of the consumers here.
- With excellent quality fabrics that are both comfortable and at the same time easy to maintain are another added benefits.
- Premium Salwar Kameez have the potential of acceptance as party wear dresses as well.

Features	Benefits
Uniqueness (Indianness)	New cultural and traditional exposure
Comfortable Fitting	Easy to carry
Trendy	Socially acclaimed

Price

Namaste INDIA

- For setting the prices of our product, we shall be adopting a Value based pricing strategy.
- Medium Range Salwar Kameez- beautified with light embroidery. Apt for office work and casual wear. (€ 45-€60)
- Heavy Range Salwar Kameez- Especially designed for parties. (€60-€70)
- Exclusive Range Salwar Kameez- embroidery with unique design or as desired by the customer. (€ 80 and above)

Place

- The outlet has been located very near to the University of Cologne to exploit the market that the University offers.
- With the number of students walking across the place, word of mouth shall defiantly spread the product talk far and across.

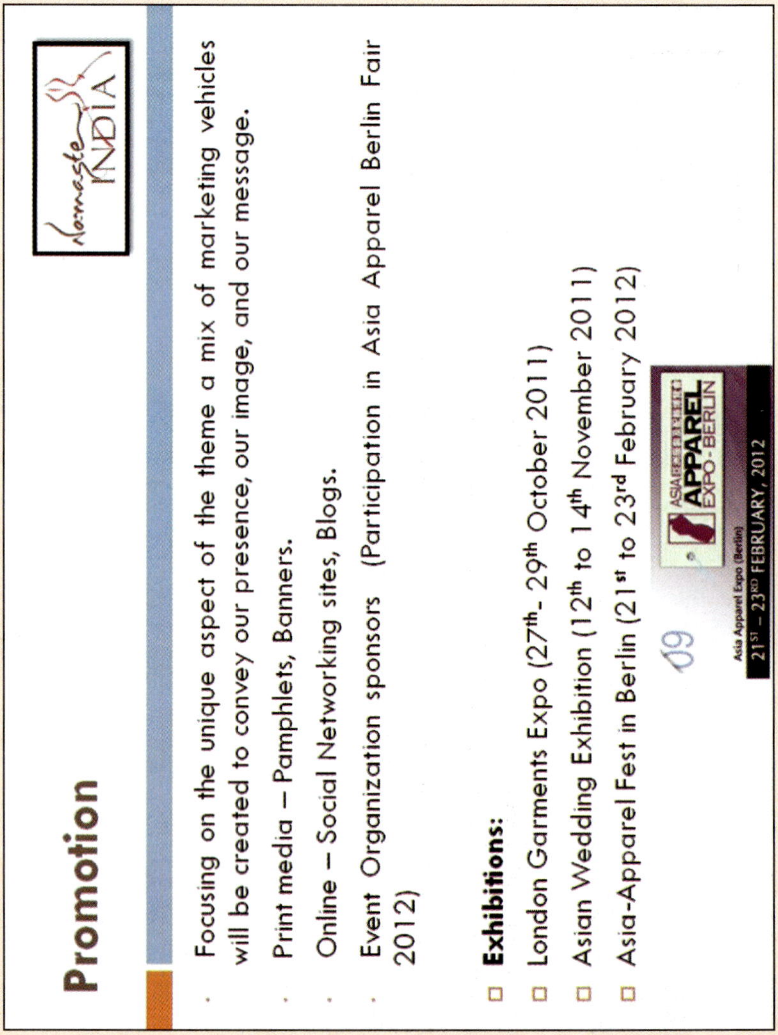
Promotion
Namaste INDIA
Focusing on the unique aspect of the theme a mix of marketing vehicles will be created to convey our presence, our image, and our message.
Print media – Pamphlets, Banners.
Online – Social Networking sites, Blogs.
Event Organization sponsors (Participation in Asia Apparel Berlin Fair 2012)
Exhibitions:
London Garments Expo (27th- 29th October 2011)
Asian Wedding Exhibition (12th to 14th November 2011)
Asia-Apparel Fest in Berlin (21st to 23rd February 2012)
APPAREL EXPO - BERLIN
Asia Apparel Expo (Berlin)
21ST – 23RD FEBRUARY, 2012

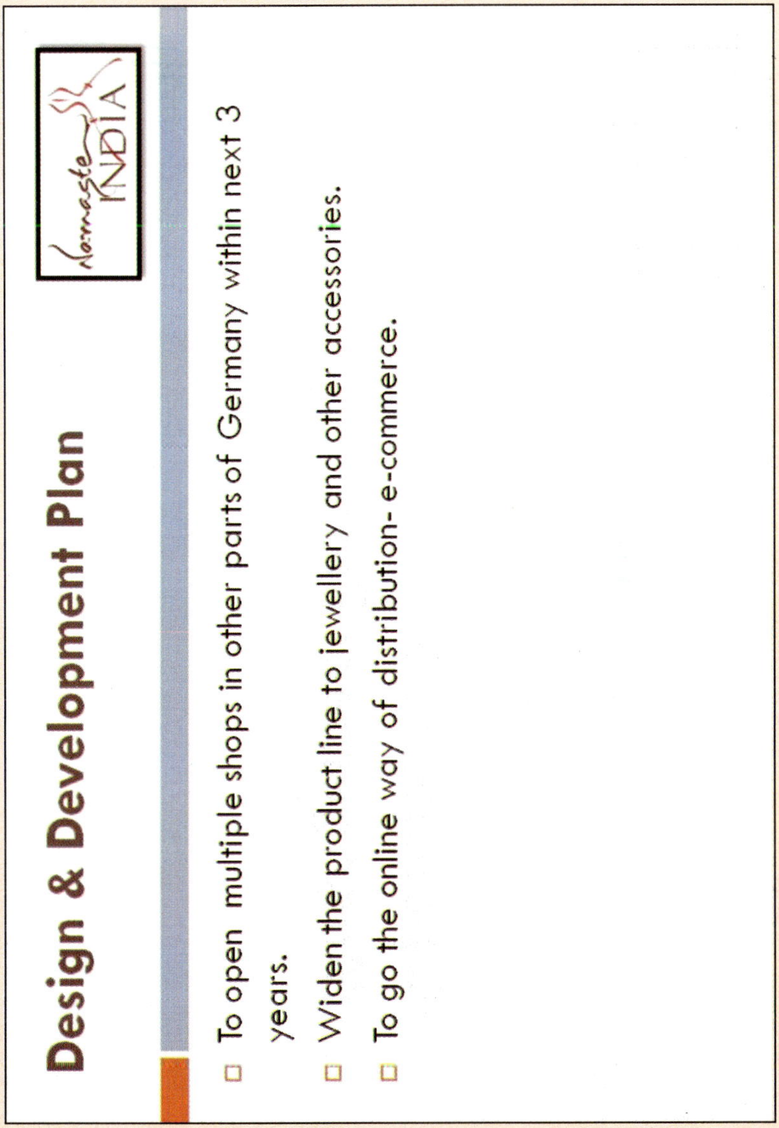
Design & Development Plan
Namaste INDIA
To open multiple shops in other parts of Germany within next 3 years.
Widen the product line to jewellery and other accessories.
To go the online way of distribution- e-commerce.

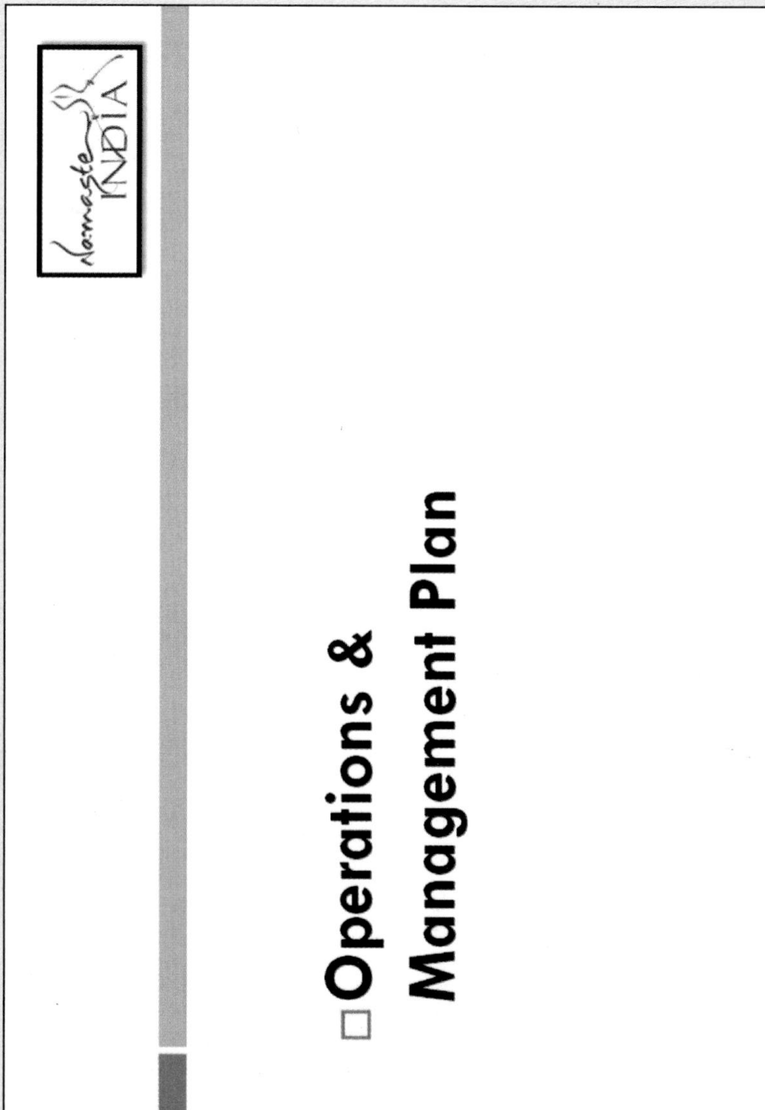
Namaste INDIA
Operations & Management Plan

Facilities

Namaste INDIA

- We plan to open a retail outlet by taking a shop space of 63 sq. m at Münstereifeler road 1 Münstereifeler Straße 1, Colgone Sulz.
- The bright retail space (approx. 26 sqm) offer useful for tailor's collection. The large window offers a glimpse of the city life and potential customers.
- Also, Sülz Cologne's with the lowest unemployment rate, which is reflected ultimately in the purchasing power and willingness to buy.

Hours of Operation

- The shop shall be open from 12:00 pm to 8:00 pm with closing times extended to 10:00 pm on Saturdays.
- The shop shall remain closed on Sundays and any other declared holidays.

Employee Training and Education

- The shop shall be run by our partner who already is trained in taking measurements and altering to small extent.

Systems and Control

- A big emphasis is being placed on extensive research into the designs and integrity of our products.
- A rigor check on the quality of cloth used, embroidery done and packing of the products shall be done in India itself and supplier is responsible for ensuring the same with constant check from us as well.
- The packing shall have fulfill 'din' standards and will also be checked for the same.
- Also, barcodes shall be used for billing as well keeping the inventory counts.

Legal Considerations

Namaste INDIA

- In our partnership contract, it shall be governed by the Indian Partnership Act 1932.
- Any disputes if and when they arise shall be addressed in the Indian Court of law.
- Also, the partnership has been formed at will, and thus its shall be continued as per the will of the partners based on their mutual understanding.

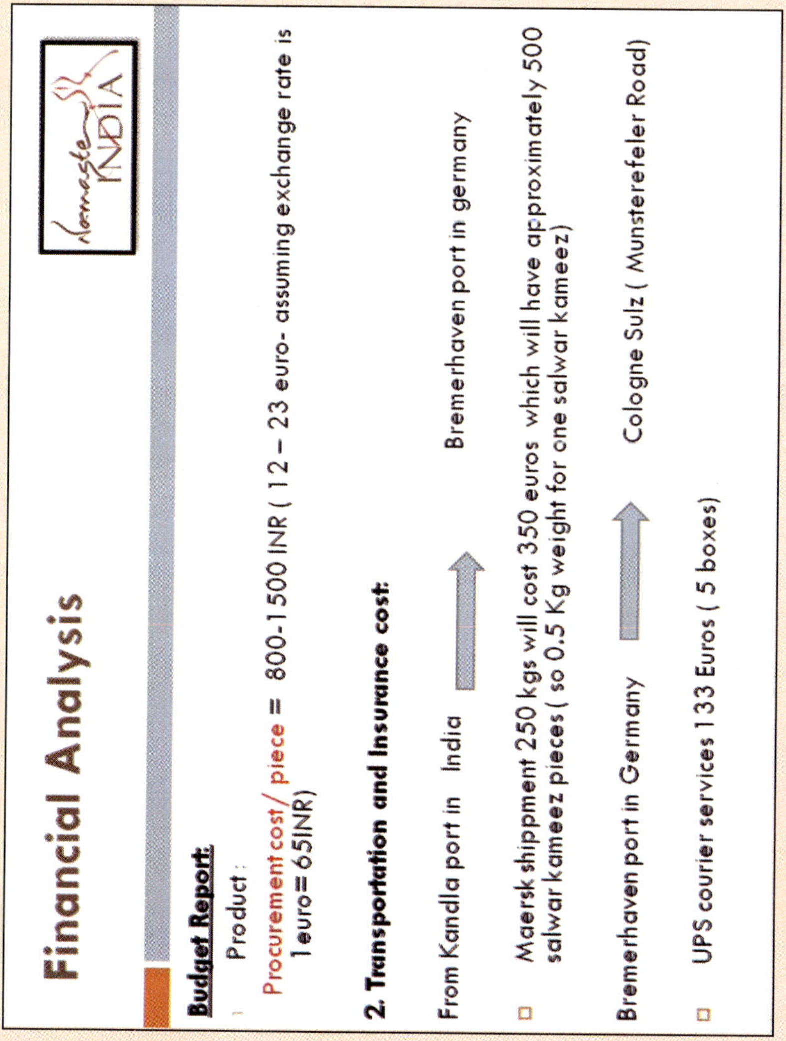
Financial Analysis
Budget Report:
Product :
Procurement cost/ piece = 800-1500 INR (12 – 23 euro- assuming exchange rate is 1 euro= 65INR)
2. Transportation and Insurance cost:
From Kandla port in India
Bremerhaven port in germany
Maersk shippment 250 kgs will cost 350 euros which will have approximately 500 salwar kameez pieces (so 0.5 Kg weight for one salwar kameez)
Bremerhaven port in Germany
Cologne Sulz (Munsterefeler Road)
UPS courier services 133 Euros (5 boxes)

3. Store Rent and insurance

- Rent for the store will be 820 per month euros inclusive of water and electricity
- Insurance for the store is 100 euro s per year.

4. **Fixed cost of setting up the store:**

- Billing machine: 89 euro
- Bar code reader- 59 euro
- Computers- Available
- Chairs – free
- Billies- 116 euros (4* 29 euros per piece)
- Cloth Rails- 30 euros (5* 6 Euros per piece)
- Maniquinn-100 euros (2 * 50 euros per piece)
- Rent – 820 euro s per month (820* 12= 9840 euro s per year)
- Insurance- 100 euros per year

Total Fixed cost - 10334 euros

Total Recurring expenses

- Raw materials- 12-23 euros per piece (**we assume that in the first year we are selling 4150 units)**
- Marketing and advt - 81 euros (6000 pamphlets printing) (source- dieuwelt druckerei)

PER UNIT = 81/6000= .0135 EUROS PER PAMPHLET

- Transportation - 483 euros per shipment OF 500 UNITS (350+ 133)

Per unit= 500/483 = 1.036 euros per unit

- **Total Variable cost per unit= 12-23 euros +/- 1.5 euros**

Namaste INDIA
Assuming that we sell 4150 units per year in the first year of operation:
Selling price per unit:
1. Light embroidary and work- 45-60 euros per piece
2. Heavy embroidary – 60-80 euros per piece
Total sales :
Best case: 4150* 60 = 249000
Pessimistic case : 4150* 45 = 186750

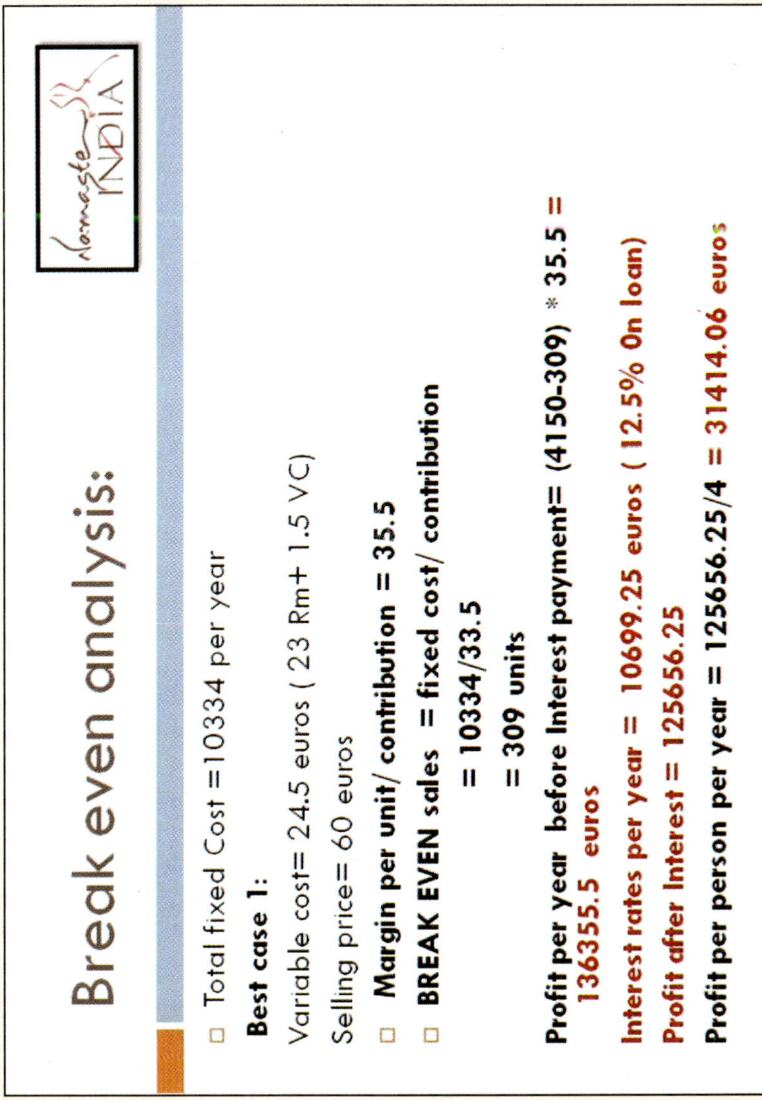
Break even analysis:
Total fixed Cost =10334 per year
Best case 1:
Variable cost= 24.5 euros (23 Rm+ 1.5 VC)
Selling price= 60 euros
Margin per unit/ contribution = 35.5
BREAK EVEN sales = fixed cost/ contribution
= 10334/33.5
= 309 units
Profit per year before Interest payment= (4150-309) * 35.5 = 136355.5 euros
Interest rates per year = 10699.25 euros (12.5% 0n loan)
Profit after Interest = 125656.25
Profit per person per year = 125656.25/4 = 31414.06 euros
Namaste INDIA

Case 2 Worst case:

- Total fixed cost = 10334 per year
- Variable cost= 13.5 euros (12 Rm+ 1.5 VC)
- Selling price = 45 euros
- Margin Per unit/ contribution = 31.5
- Break even point = fixed cost/ Contribution
  = 10334/ 31.5
  = 329units

Profit per year before interest rates = (4150-329) * 31.5 = 120361.5 euros

Interest rates per year = 10699.25 euros (12.5% 0n loan)

Profit after Interest = (120361.5-10699.25) = 109662.25

Profit per person per year = 109662.25/4 = 27515.56 euros

Financing

- From SIDBI (Small Industries Development Bank Of India) at an interest rate of 12.5%

Loan amount = 85594 Euros

Interest = **10699.25 Euros**

Other Selling Points

- **At the Flea Markets:**
- Flohmarkt Schaumainkai (Frankfurt)
- At the Frankfurt flea market you can buy all sorts of handicrafts/textiles. The market takes place at Schaumainkai between Eiserner Steg and Holbeinsteg.
- Opening hours: Sat (except for national holidays) 9 am – 2 pm

Partner Restaurants:

- **Cologne:**
- Buy-Buy Restaurant
- Royal Punjab
- Mumbai Palace

- **Dusseldorf:**
- Delhi Haat
- Mayur
- Tandoori

- **Frankfurt**
- Lahore Kebab Haus

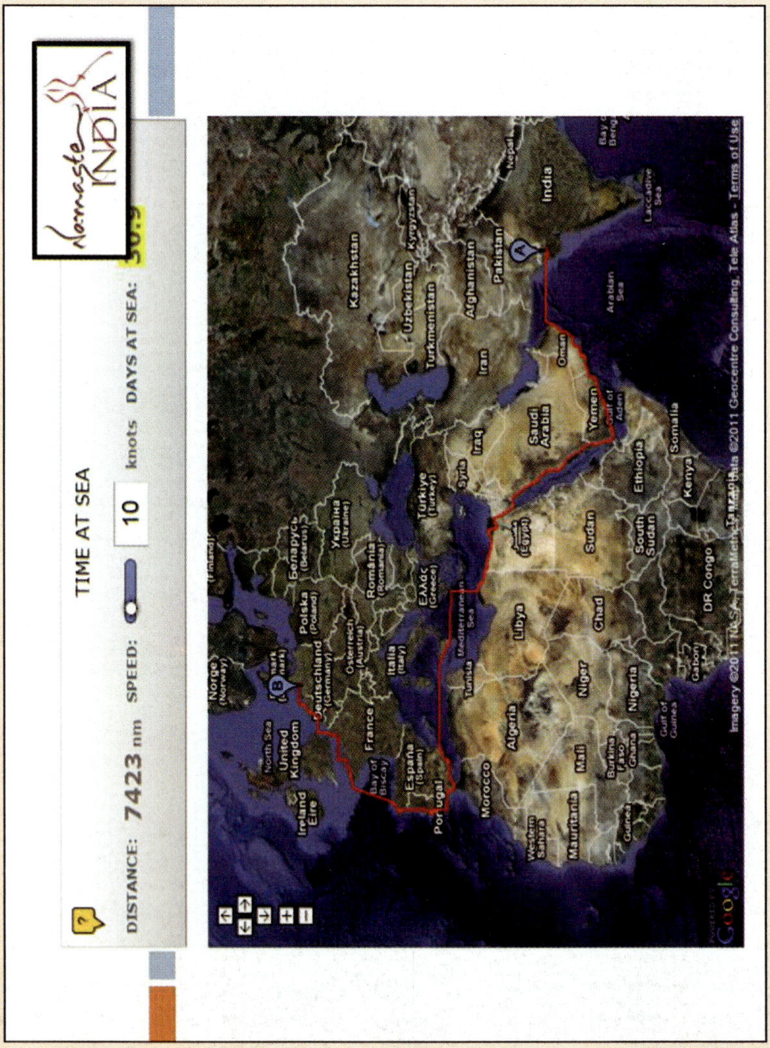
Namaste INDIA
TIME AT SEA
DISTANCE: 7423 nm
SPEED: 10 knots
DAYS AT SEA:

See also: *Districts of Cologne*

District	Population					
	Population (1990)	Population (1995)	Population (2000)	Population (2005)	Population (2009)	Population (2025)[estimated]
1. Innenstadt	137.283	138.637 ▲	133.454 ▼	129.496 ▼	126.301 ▼	*128.400* ▲
2. Rodenkirchen	91.284	94.582 ▲	97.790 ▲	100.490 ▲	100.827 ▲	*110.500* ▲
3. Lindenthal	134.823	135.276 ▲	139.026 ▲	139.803 ▲	137.870 ▼	*145.300* ▲
4. Ehrenfeld	95.243	95.552 ▲	97.396 ▲	102.939 ▲	103.708 ▲	*105.900* ▲
5. Nippes	111.133	109.481 ▼	108.206 ▼	109.235 ▲	111.141 ▲	*111.000* ▼
6. Chorweiler	74.481	79.073 ▲	83.215 ▲	82.865 ▼	80.459 ▼	*77.700* ▼
7. Porz	100.695	105.433 ▲	107.447 ▲	106.647 ▼	106.533 ▼	*107.000* ▲
8. Kalk	108.769	108.185 ▼	106.377 ▼	107.194 ▲	109.045 ▲	*105.800* ▼
9. Mülheim	142.889	141.877 ▼	144.321 ▲	144.432 ▲	144.419 ▼	*140.300* ▼
Cologne	**998.590** ▼	**1.008.848** ▲	**1.017.721** ▲	**1.023.101** ▲	**1.020.303** ▼	***1.031.800*** ▲

districts of Cologne

See also: *Census in Germany* and *Immigration to Germany*

District	Population (2009)	German citizens			Foreign citizens							
		(total)	German citizens w/o migration backgr.	German citizens w/ migration backgr.	(total)	from inside the EU[1]	from Turkey	from elsewhere in Europe	from Africa[2]	from the Americas	from Asia[3]	from elsewhere
1. Innenstadt	126.301	104.945	92.946	11.999	21.356	9.524	4.502	2.532	924	1.287	2.460	127
2. Rodenkirchen	100.827	86.823	74.938	11.885	14.004	5.717	3.298	1.850	827	505	1.747	60
3. Lindenthal	137.870	124.943	111.586	13.357	12.927	6.034	1.600	1.646	627	762	2.146	112
4. Ehrenfeld	103.708	83.614	69.749	13.865	20.094	6.824	7.960	2.394	970	459	1.367	120
5. Nippes	111.141	91.048	77.230	13.818	20.093	5.876	9.584	2.131	857	409	1.146	90
6. Chorweiler	80.459	65.770	46.806	18.964	14.689	3.216	6.989	2.589	456	96	1.252	91
7. Porz	106.533	91.368	71.409	19.959	15.165	4.802	4.412	3.178	653	196	1.850	75
8. Kalk	109.045	82.012	61.387	20.625	27.033	6.867	10.865	4.287	1.772	280	1.772	108
9. Mülheim	144.419	116.935	93.804	23.131	27.484	6.642	12.480	3.885	1.750	443	2.202	82
Cologne	**1.020.303**	**847.458**	**699.855**	**147.603**	**172.845**	**55.502**	**61.690**	**24.492**	**8.835**	**4.437**	**17.024**	**865**

[1] largest groups from Italy, Poland and Greece

[2] largest group from Morocco

[3] largest group from Iran

Keupstraße in the district of Mülheim is a centre of the Turkish community in Cologne.

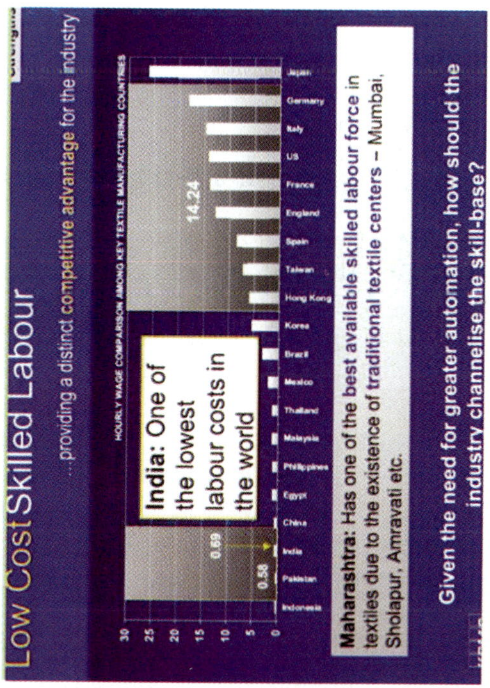
Low Cost Skilled Labour
...providing a distinct competitive advantage for the industry
HOURLY WAGE COMPARISON AMONG KEY TEXTILE MANUFACTURING COUNTRIES
India: One of the lowest labour costs in the world
14.24
0.69
0.58
Indonesia
Pakistan
India
China
Egypt
Philippines
Malaysia
Thailand
Mexico
Brazil
Korea
Hong Kong
Taiwan
Spain
England
France
US
Italy
Germany
Japan
Maharashtra: Has one of the best available skilled labour force in textiles due to the existence of traditional textile centers – Mumbai, Sholapur, Amravati etc.
Given the need for greater automation, how should the industry channelise the skill-base?

Bibliography

Achtenhagen, Frank (1997), Berufliche Ausbildung. In: *Weinert, Franz E.* [ed.], Enzyklopädie der Psychologie – Psychologie des Unterrichts und der Schule [Themenbereich D – Praxisgebiete, Serie I –Pädagogische Psychologie, vol. 3], Göttingen etc, pp. 603-657.

Achtenhagen, Frank et al. (1992), *Lernhandeln in komplexen Situationen – Neue Konzepte der betriebswirtschaftlichen Ausbildung*, Wiesbaden.

Barr, R. B.; Tagg, J (1995), From Teaching to Learning: A New Paradigm for Undergraduate Education. In: *Change*, 27, No. 6, pp. 12-25

Buddensiek, Wilfried (1992), Entscheidungstraining im Methodenverbund – Didaktische Begründung für die Verbindung von Fallstudie und Simulationsspiel. In: *Keim, Helmut* [ed.], Planspiel-Rollenspiel-Fallstudie – Zur Praxis und Theorie lernaktiver Methoden, Köln, pp. 9-24.

Copeland, M. T. (1954), The Genesis of the Case Method in Business Instruction. In: McNair, M. P. [ed.], The *Case Method at the Harvard Business School*. Papers by present and past members of the faculty and staff. New York, McGraw-Hill, pp. 25–33.

Dubs, Rolf (1989), Vernetztes Denken im Wirtschaftslehreunterricht. In: *Zeitschrift für Berufs- und Wirtschaftspädagogik*, Vol. 85, No. 1, pp. 50-61.

Dubs, Rolf (1996), Komplexe Lehr-Lern-Arrangements im Wirtschaftsunterricht. Grundlagen, Gestaltungsprinzipien und Verwendung im Unterricht. In: *Beck, Klaus et al.* [eds.], Berufserziehung im Umbruch – Didaktische Herausforderungen und Ansätze zu ihrer Bewältigung [Festschrift for J. Zabeck], Weinheim, pp. 159-172.

Erskine, J. A., Leenders, M. R., & Mauffette-Leenders, L. A. (2003). *Teaching with cases*. London, Ontario: Ivey Publ., Richard Ivey School of Business.

Hofstede, Geert (1980), Culture's Consequences, International Differences in *Work-Related Values*, Beverly Hills/London, SAGE Publications.

Hofstede, Geert (1986), Cultural Differences in Teaching and Learning. In: *International Journal of Intercultural Relations*, Vol. 10, pp. 301 – 320.

Jackson, J. (2001), Cross-Cultural Case Discussions in International Business, In: *Journal of Teaching in International Business*, 13:1, pp. 67-86.

John, Ernst G. (1992), Fallstudien und Fallstudienunterricht. In: Achtenhagen, Frank; John, Ernst G. [eds.], Mehrdimensionale Lehr-Lern-Arrangements –Innovationen in der kaufmännischen Aus- und Weiterbildung, Wiesbaden, pp. 79-91.

Kaiser, Franz-Josef (1983), Grundlagen der Fallstudiendidaktik – Historische Entwicklung-Theoretische Grundlagen-Unterrichtliche Praxis. In: *Kaiser, Franz-Josef* [ed.], Die Fallstudie –Theorie und Praxis der Fallstudiendidaktik, Bad Heilbrunn, pp. 9-34.

Kaiser, Franz-Josef (1992), Der Beitrag aktiver partizipativer Methoden Fallstudie, Rollenspiel und Planspiel zur Vermittlung von Schlüsselqualifikationen. In: *Keim, Helmut* [ed.], Planspiel-Rollenspiel-Fallstudie –Zur Praxis und Theorie lernaktiver Methoden, Köln, pp. 62-90.

Kaiser, Franz-Josef; Kaminski, Hans (1994), *Methodik des Ökonomie-Unterrichts – Grundlagen eines handlungsorientierten Lernkonzepts mit Beispielen*, Bad Heilbrunn.

Keim, Helmut (1992), Zur kategorialen Klassifikation von Fallstudie, Rollen- und Planspiel. In: *Keim, Helmut* [ed.], Planspiel-Rollenspiel-Fallstudie – Zur Praxis und Theorie lernaktiver Methoden, Köln, pp. 122-151.

Kell, Adolf; van Buer, Jürgen; Schneider, Dagmar (1992), Probleme der pädagogischen Beurteilung komplexer Lehr-Lern-Arrangements. In: *Achtenhagen, Frank*; John, Ernst G. [eds.], Mehr-dimensionale Lehr-Lern-Arrangements – Innovationen in der kaufmännischen Aus- und Weiter-bildung, Wiesbaden, pp. 511-547.

Leenders, M. R., Mauffette-Leenders, L. A., & Erskine, J. A. (2001). *Writing cases* (4th ed.). London, Ontario: Ivey Publ., Richard Ivey School of Business.

Manikutty, Sankaran; Anuradha, N.S. und Hansen, Katrin (2007), Does culture influence learning styles in higher education? In: *International Journal of Learning and Change*, 2 (1). pp. 70-87.

Marton, F.; Säljö, R. (1976), On qualitative Differences in Learning. I – Outcome and Process, In: *British Journal of Educational Psychology* 46, pp. 4-11.

Mauffette-Leenders, L. A., Erskine, J. A., & Leenders, M. R. (2005). *Learning with cases*. London, Ontario: Ivey Publ., Richard Ivey School of Business.

Palfreyman, David; McBride, Dawn Lorraine (2007), *Learning and Teaching across Cultures in Higher Education*, New York, Palgrave Macmillan.

Pilz, Matthias (2002b), Vom Lernen über Modelle zum Lernen am Modell. In: *Unterricht Wirtschaft*, Vol. 3, no. 11 [3rd quarter, 2002], pp. 36-39

Pilz, Matthias (2008), Fallstudie. In: Hedtke, Reinhold; Weber, Brigitte [ed.], Wörterbuch ökonomische Bildung, Schwalbach, Wochenschau-Verlag, pp. 123f.

Pilz, Matthias et al. (2003), Leitfaden für die Erstellung von Ausbildungseinheiten (AE). In: *Schweizerische Zeitschrift für das kaufmännische Bildungswesen*, Vol. 97, No. 1, pp. 28-47.

Pilz, Roland (1971), Der wirtschaftskundliche praxisbezogene Fall als Mittel zur inneren Differenzierung. In: *Wirtschaft und Erziehung*, Vol. 23, No. 9, pp. 204-206.

Pilz, Roland (1972), Problemlösendes Lernen am wirtschaftskundlichen praxisbezogenen Fall. In: *Wirtschaft und Erziehung*, Vol. 24, No. 11, pp. 278-281.

Pilz, Roland (1978), Entscheidungsorientierte Unterrichtsgestaltung durch Einsatz des wirtschaftskundlichen praxisbezogenen Falls. In: *Zeitschrift für Berufs- und Wirtschaftspädagogik*, Vol. 74, No. 2, pp. 95-110.

Preiß, Peter (1992), Komplexität im Betriebswirtschaftslehre-Anfangsunterricht. In: *Achtenhagen, Frank*; John, Ernst G. [ed.], *Mehrdimensionale Lehr-Lern-Arrangements –Innovationen in der kaufmännischen Aus- und Weiterbildung*, Wiesbaden, pp. 58-78.

Reetz, Lothar (1984), Wirtschaftsdidaktik –Eine Einführung in *Theorie und Praxis wirtschaftsberuflicher Curriculumentwicklung und Unterrichtsgestaltung*, Bad Heilbrunn

Reetz, Lothar (1988a), Zum Einsatz didaktischer Fallstudien im Wirtschaftslehreunterricht. In: *Unterrichtswissenschaft*, Vol. 16, No. 2, pp. 38-55.

Reetz, Lothar (1988b), Fälle und Fallstudien im Wirtschaftslehre-Unterricht. In: *Wirtschaft und Erziehung*, Vol. 40, No. 5, pp. 148-156.

Reetz, Lothar (1992), Curriculumentwicklung und entdeckendes Lernen mit Hilfe von Fallstudien. In: Achtenhagen, Frank; John, Ernst G. [eds.], *Mehrdimensionale Lehr-Lern-Arrangements – Innovationen in der kaufmännischen Aus- und Weiterbildung*, Wiesbaden, pp. 340-352.

Reetz, Lothar; Sievers, Hans-Peter (1983), Zur curriculum- und lerntheoretischen Begründung der Fallstudienverwendung im Wirtschaftslehreunterricht der Sekundarstufe II. In: Kaiser, Franz-Josef [ed.], *Die Fallstudie –Theorie und Praxis der Fallstudiendidaktik*, Bad Heilbrunn, pp. 75-110.

Stark, Robin et al. (1995), Förderung von Handlungskompetenz durch geleitetes Problemlösen und multiple Lernkontexte. In: *Zeitschrift für Entwicklungspsychologie und Pädagogische Psychologie*, Vol. XXVII, No. 4, pp. 289-312

Waibel, Roland (1996), Unterrichtsbeispiel: Einführung in das Unternehmensmodell anhand der Methodik des vernetzten Denkens. In: *Zeitschrift für Berufs- und Wirtschaftspädagogik*, Vol. 92, No. 1, pp. 46-55

Wolf, Karl (1992), Die Fallstudie als Unterrichtsmethode, ein Plädoyer. In: *Wirtschaft und Erziehung*, Vol. 44, No. 5, pp. 158f.